I AM NOT FORGOTTEN
GOD KNOWS MY NAME

A personal journal by
Clara Stephens

WOMEN FOR CHRIST
INTERNATIONAL FOUNDATION
WFCIF.ORG

Foreword

Every believer has a **destiny** in God: an ultimate picture or attainment in life outlining purpose and reinforcing fulfilment. The journey to destiny is never an easy route. Though sure, but inevitably laden with pains, plights, contests, ordeals and lures. These are processes in destiny making.

As destiny varies with individuals, the process or encounters evolving it differ too.

Invariably, process is not vicious; being means to ordained aspiration or future. Worth mentioning however is our attitude towards it. We are either upbeat and confident or upset, nerved and distant.

With negative outlook, we are incensed, tensed, impatient, distressed and panic. We develop a fright and flight mentality. Life is viewed unfair, unfriendly, rough and reprehensive. On this track, we misunderstand **process**, react poorly to it and short-circuit intended effect: destiny realisation.

However, a positive response to process reveals a mind set on intended outcome, with appropriate alignment. Life challenges are viewed as component for destiny preparation and fulfilment and call for courage and patience as long as they last. Strong character is built and destiny is forged.

The Author in this work recounts her life tales, practise and understanding of purpose, demonstrating positive response to process that births it.

The narrations were down to earth, encounters were unimaginably inhuman, sordid, and undignifying but courage and patience had the better valour.

She was cheated, dejected and humiliated. Stoutly, she kept a calm disposition. Her teachable spirit and deference to counsel leveraged on divine strength and victory for her. She was rewarded. Everything fell into shape. Life now has a meaning; desires, pictures and dreams of life are established.

By implication, godly desires or life dreams are possible and predicated on positive attitude to processes involved. Attitude is life. How an individual responds makes all the difference. The disquieting moments one may encounter now are not unconnected. They are part of life processes to bring fulfilment and establish destiny. For all the years the author has been part of our ministry, she has always trusted God, been patient, till her breakthrough came.

I recommend this great book from my daughter in faith to all who acknowledge there is hope in their future, and future in their hope. What you are going through will not see your end; you will see their end. As she, uncompromisingly made it through righteous principles, on same track, you will make it.

Seeing you on the sunny side of life.

Dr Tunde Bakare
Serving Overseer
The Latter Rain Assembly
Lagos, Nigeria.

Dedication

To God for being God and God alone in my life.

Acknowledgements

- My husband Paul for his love, patience, and for believing in me.
- Pastor and Mrs. Tunde Bakare of *Latter Rain Ministries*, Lagos, Nigeria. I am so very thankful for the care and direction you have both given to me through the years. Furthermore, your call to all nations, to develop and restore churches to the biblical pattern, encourages me to believe God for more in my life – to not be satisfied with the way things are.
- The members and partners of *Latter Rain Ministries*. Thank you for supporting the vision and making it possible for many lives, mine included, to be transformed by the Word of God.
- Pastor Jentezen Franklin and his wife Cherise of *Free Chapel Church* in Gainesville, Georgia. For your humility and the opportunity to use the gift of God in my life to serve and to grow in the church.
- Apostle Jamie T. and Kimberly Pleasant of the *Kingdom Builder Christian Center* in Norcross, Georgia.
- Pastors Bank and Sharon Akinmola of *World Outreach for All Nations Church*, Atlanta, Georgia.
- Pastors James and Faith Iruofagar, originally from Lagos, Nigeria, who moved to the United States to birth another church.

- Dr. Jonathan David and his wife Helen of the *Full Gospel Centre* in Muar Johor, Malaysia.
- Dr. Delron Shirley and his wife Peggy of *Teach All Nations Ministry*, located in Colorado Springs, Colorado.

Table of Contents

Dedication vii
Acknowledgements.. ix
Introduction... xiii
Part I
    Chapter One: The Road to Destiny 15
    Chapter Two: Wrong Way?...21
    Chapter Three: That I May Know Him.......................29
    Chapter Four: A Ray of Hope 37
    Chapter Five: Jesus, My Connection 43
    Chapter Six: Highs and Lows 53
    Chapter Seven: Doubts, Triumphs, and Temptations...65
    Chapter Eight: God's Reward 73
    Chapter Nine: A Change of Plans 87
    Chapter Ten: No Progress without Process.................99
    Chapter Eleven: Jobs Are Not Scarce; Faithful
        Men Are 107
Appendix A: Work for the Lord...................................... 111
Appendix B: A Christian Employee's Motto 113
Appendix C: A Few Questions to Ponder 115
Notes 117
Postscript...119
Author Contact Information...121

Introduction

I write this book as a testament of God's goodness and mercy in my life, and I give Him all the glory for giving me the grace to finally share my personal journey. It is my earnest prayer that my life story will encourage the weary, strengthen the weak, and lead lost sheep back home. Above all, however, my desire is for every reader to know beyond a shadow of doubt that God is a God of purpose and that He does everything according to His plan. He orders the steps of the righteous and rewards those who diligently seek Him.

Throughout my life I have experienced God's leading and direction in every situation, and His Holy Spirit is and has always been my guide. Therefore, I pray that you will allow the Holy Spirit to speak to your heart as you read my story. Perhaps you have been struggling with issues and situations that threaten to consume you. Maybe you feel lonely and without help. I am here to tell you that God is always there, waiting for you to invite Him into your life. He is more than willing to help. *How do I know?* I am a living witness!

I considered sharing my story using a pseudonym but realized that I could not do so; I had to be completely open and honest. However, wanting to protect the identities of others who have been mentioned, many names have been changed. The exception to this is the ministers and ministries that God has used to help me nurture my faith and build a firm foundation in Him.

<u>Isaiah 33:5-6</u>
The LORD is exalted, for he dwells on high; he will fill Zion with justice and righteousness. He will be the sure foundation for your times, a rich store of salvation and wisdom and knowledge; the fear of the LORD is the key to this treasure.

Chapter One

The Road to Destiny

Sometimes we look at successful people and desire to be like them. We may even feel a little envious of their success. It seems as if life has smiled favorably on them. However, if we were to take the time to talk to them and find out the process that got them there, many of us might not be willing to pay such a price.

My story is no different. I did not enter this world with a *silver spoon* in my mouth. Rather, I was born in Nigeria, West Africa, the fifth of eight children, and was raised by two very hard-working and enterprising parents. My father was a farmer and trader who traveled extensively, selling his products from state to state. My mother owned a multi-purpose shop that would be the equivalent to a mid-sized Wal-Mart.

Basically, my family was all about business. We ate it, drank it, slept it. In fact, I do not remember a time when business was not uppermost in the minds of both my parents.

My father firmly believed that one must not be caught idle or sleeping during the day. He would wake up my five brothers, two sisters, and me at the crack of dawn. Then, he would put us through rigorous training: sweeping the yard, fetching water, or stocking the shop. Even if there were no work to be done, he would get us up any way just to sit down because as he put it, "Poverty befalls those who sleep until sunrise." I later found out that what he said was a Biblical principle:

Proverbs 6: 10-11
A little sleep, a little slumber, a little folding of the hands to rest—and poverty will come on you like a bandit and scarcity like an armed man.

Clara finisher of ATC marathon & half 08

My father also taught each of us his trade. We would walk ten miles to and from his farm a couple of times per week where we learned how to both sow seed and harvest crops. Then, when we reached a certain age my father put each of us to work selling produce in nearby towns. I was 10 years old when I began.

All of my training paid off! In the true spirit of my father I eventually started my own business. I would go to the farms very early in the morning to buy vegetables at a discounted price. As soon as school finished for the day, I would hawk everything I had purchased for a profit. I was always happy to increase my savings.

My mother was a very spiritual woman with a deep love for the Lord. And just as much as my father believed in getting up early and working, my mother believed the Biblical proverb: "Train a child in the way he should go, and when he is old he will not turn from it" (22:6). She enrolled me in the church choir, Bible study for youth, and the Girls' Brigade (similar to Girl Scouts). In fact, what with my church activities and our family businesses I had little time to play like some of the neighborhood kids!

◆

As I grew older my father was away more and more on business trips. In fact, most of the time, Mom had to raise us children all by herself. *Can you imagine trying to keep track of six very active children while running a large business and a house?* Now that I am a wife and mother, I can better understand how difficult it must have been.

Being the "single" mother while my father traveled was very trying for several reasons. However, one in particular stands out. It soon became impossible for Mom to monitor all of our movements. My brothers and I just did what we pleased, and that was not a good thing! For example, with little supervision and a whole lot of money my eldest brother began experimenting with drugs. When Mom found out, she sank into a deep depression. She must have felt responsible; it was just too much for her to handle.

My brother's decision also affected me but in a different way. I helplessly watched as my family began to slowly fall apart. It was then that I decided something very important — I wanted to be different from my brothers. I would lie on my bed, studying my Bible and asking God for help. Often, I would cry myself to sleep.

Psalm 107:13
Then they cried to the Lord in their trouble, and he saved them from their distress.

God answered my prayers; He revealed Himself to me. It happened one day at a Girls' Brigade meeting. I heard a voice, saying "I will never leave you to wander alone. I will be with you always."

Immediately, I experienced an instant change. It was as if a new person had taken up residence in me. At that moment I even felt so weak that I collapsed! My friends picked me up, but I was too afraid to tell them what had just transpired. I suddenly became very quiet and gentle. *What a change that was!* Until that moment I had been a very talkative girl who would yell, shout, and even curse.

2 Corinthians 5:17
Therefore, if anyone is in Christ, he is a new creation; the old has gone, the new has come!

When I got home, I tried to explain to my Mom what had happened to me but just ended up apologizing for every wrong I had ever done to her. I promised I would never be rude nor curse people out ever again. She could not get over how calm and quiet I had become. My mom still remembers that evening vividly; even today, years later, she talks about it!

That day I became a new creation. Everything about me changed for the better. I began to mature physically and spiritually. I loved the Lord more than anything. I was very active in the church and was allowed to sing in the adult choir. I led the Girls' Brigade youth club and was involved in Bible study and drama groups as well.

◆

But even though I had become a Christian, life still had its challenges. One of the biggest for me was that I was growing up in the midst of five boys, four older and one younger. Being the only girl—my sisters had not been born yet—my brothers gave me a very hard time. it seemed like they were jealous of the interest my dad showed me, and I am sure they thought I received preferential treatment from our Mom too.

My brothers would wait until our parents were out and then gang up on me. They would call a "boys only" time and exclude me from their activities. Often I was forced to walk several steps behind them on the way to the farm. It was as if they were trying to get even in any and every way possible. Their treatment made me feel lonely and rejected

However, being by myself so much of the time also gave me the opportunity to grow stronger spiritually. The Holy Spirit became my Companion, my Comforter, and my Strength. As I studied God's Word, my love for Him deepened. I wanted to know Him more each day. I would pray, asking Him to use me and give me lots of wisdom.

The Lord became my confidant; I shared all my dreams and aspirations with Him. I was planning to be a well-educated, successful business woman who owned my own car and house. Everything my father did, I wanted to do double!

◆

I finished elementary school at the age of eleven. Then, I was admitted to a high school in another town called Odo-Ere, in Kwara State; it was a boarding school. Once there I joined the Athletic Club and the Literary/Debating Society — determined to be a stand-out student, to make my mark.

I did not want to embarrass my family or let anyone down. Two of my older brothers had already entered the same school before I did, but one had been expelled a year prior to my admission when he had become involved with a gang. I felt powerless to do anything about my brothers, but I wanted everyone to know that I was different.

I clung on to God with all my might, with the assurance that He was my only hope.

Chapter Two

Wrong Way?

Sometimes when driving somewhere, we may get to a point where it becomes suddenly clear that we are traveling down the wrong road. When that happens, all we have to do is to turn around and retrace our steps to see where we missed it or perhaps ask someone for better directions. It's as easy as that!

However, the road to destiny is very different. It may seem as if we are on the wrong track because the road comes with painful twists and turns. We may even question God's wisdom in allowing us to go that way! Oftentimes, however, it turns out that the road we loathe the most often (you know, the one with no shortcuts) is our must-travel route.

◆

Personally, I was very excited when I started secondary school. I felt as if I were on the right track toward realizing my dreams of becoming a well educated, successful business woman. Impressed and inspired by those professionals I met through my father's ventures, my desire was to become like them or even better. So, I worked hard at my studies.

Everything seemed to be falling into place nicely when my life took an interesting turn at the end of my first year. That's when my Dad's recently divorced brother suddenly returned from the United Kingdom and settled in Ibadan, a very large city with a long and colorful history. Uncle Tony chose that particular town because he had secured a position at the Ibadan Polytechnic as the Chief Architect. He was to be in charge of the housing, building, and renovations departments.

Uncle Tony did not move home by himself. He brought his daughters with him. Tyra and Monique were three and one respectively. As one could easily imagine, my Uncle Tony's hands were full with two little girls and a full time job. So, he asked my parents if I could come and help him during the summer while I was off from school.

My parents agreed, and I left with my uncle. My mom had just had another baby girl, making it eight children altogether (their seventh child, my first sister, had been born a couple of years earlier). Little did I know that was the last time I would ever live in their home!

My parents and I both thought my visit with Uncle Tony would be for the duration of my holiday only. However, to my dismay I would not be allowed to return home for the next seven years. Not even for a visit! *Why?* I became the answer to all of Uncle Tony's problems.

For, you see, I was not the first "helper" to live with my uncle since his return from London. He had had four house helpers before me, one of them Uncle Tony's widowed sister. Nobody had been able to live with him successfully because of the never ending work. However, being as young as I was and a family member, he was able to keep me there, indefinitely.

◆

Uncle Tony lived in a four bedroom apartment on the second floor of the staff quarters at the Polytechnic campus. I still remember being shown around the day of my arrival. I was told which rooms and areas of the house were restricted to me, and I received a warning not to be caught stealing anything from the rooms. I was told that I would be sharing a room with the two girls even though there were enough bedrooms for each of us to have our own.

When I was taken to my new living area, I found a large pile of dirty laundry in the middle of the floor. It was so high; I could have sworn it was at least five foot tall!

However, I was not disturbed by the pile of clothes. I knew Uncle Tony had had no help for a long time. "I can wash this up in one day," I thought to myself.

As our little tour ended, Uncle Tony told me that my first assignment was to wash all the clothes. He then showed me some medication that I had to administer to the girls. After that, he left. It seemed as if he were there one minute and gone the next! I certainly hadn't expected him to leave – after all, it was only my first day.

I thought, "What do I know about children and medicines? Clothes, I can wash. Cleaning, no big deal. Cooking, no problem. But kids? That's my Mom's department!"

At that moment the reality of what I had gotten into hit me. I broke down crying. There I was—barely thirteen years old—having the responsibility to care for an entire house and two small children! My only consolation was that it would soon be over.

"After all, it is only for the holidays!" Or so I thought at the time.

It took me two full days just to wash those clothes because I had to wash them with my bare hands in a tub. Next, I had to line dry them. It's not what you think though. We had a washer and dryer, but Uncle Tony would not allow me to use them. So, it was an arduous task that was followed by ironing. I then had to fold or hang each piece.

Washing became a part of my daily routine for the rest of my stay with Uncle Tony, but it wasn't the only thing I had to do! My schedule went something like this. I would wake up at six in the morning to sweep and mop the floors in every room of the apartment. Immediately after finishing, I would go outside to hand wash his two cars. Then, I would go back into the house and scrub the tile in the bathrooms and kitchen. Next, I would dust, wipe clean, and polish the furniture. And that was all before breakfast!

I usually would have tea with two slices of bread. Cereal was sometimes placed on the table by Uncle Tony. It had come all the way from London, which meant that it was always expired. Often, an added surprise was found inside the box — weevils. YUCK!!! Even so, if Uncle Tony brought it to the table, I had to eat it (and them).

Breakfast was immediately followed by the washing up. Then, my uncle would give me a list of chores for the day. He always made it very clear that I was expected to have everything done before his return from work in the evening.

Once Uncle Tony was gone, I'd bathe the girls and dress them. Uncle Tony's room was next. I would clean, mop the floor, and change the sheets as quickly as possible because then came the laundry.

I usually took a break, if you could call it that, to prepare lunch. After fixing the meal and feeding the girls, I would eat. There was no time to rest — I only had until Uncle Tony came home for supper to finish everything. He always checked my work, and *God help me!* if anything on his list had not been accomplished.

At the end of the day I would do the dishes, bathe the girls again, and put them to bed between eight and nine. Then, and only then, was I finally able to sit down. This became my time to fellowship with God. I would read my Bible. (It was my only companion!) I'd cry out to God, talking to Him about each and every thing that had happened during the day. During those times I began to develop my ability to hear the Spirit of God. He was truly my Comforter and Guide.

My uncle was not one who went to church, so my church attendance was sporadic. I was only allowed to go to church when Uncle Tony felt like it. Usually, though, church would usually be over by the time I got there. So, my evenings with God were my only times of refreshing. Fellowshipping with God gave me much needed strength.

After what seemed an eternity of never-ending work, my holiday was coming to an end. You can imagine my joy at the prospect of returning home. My joy was short-lived, however, when Uncle Tony told me I was doing such a great job—better than any house help he had ever had. That being the case, he said that he was requesting that I be transferred from the secondary school in Odo-Ere to the polytechnic high school in Ibadan so that I could live with him permanently.

I could not believe what I was hearing! *Who gave him the right to make such a decision about my life? What would my parents have to say about it?*

I cried so hard that day. I was inconsolable.

Then, I talked to God about my situation. The Holy Spirit comforted me and told me it was for a purpose. God reminded me of His promise to never leave me or forsake me (Deut. 31:6; John 14:16-18; Heb. 13:5). He promised to be with me. I answered, "Yes, Lord".

<u>Joshua 1:5</u>

No one will be able to stand up against you all the days of your life. As I was with Moses, so I will be with you: I will never leave you nor forsake you.

◆

It was a good thing I had the Lord's assurance. For, life became even more difficult than it had been! I was now responsible for getting myself and the girls ready for school in addition to all of my regular chores.

I was still expected to wash both cars every morning. I never did understand that since Uncle Tony used only one car a day. Perhaps it would have been easier for me if I had been given the pleasure of riding to school in one of them, but I had to walk the 2 ½ miles to school each morning and that same 2 ½ miles home each afternoon.

School ended at 2:00 PM every day. Uncle Tony expected me – no excuses – to arrive no later than 2:30 PM. If I didn't, there were consequences. This made it almost impossible for me to make and keep friends since I had to walk faster than everyone else in order to get home in time. There were no casual "after school" strolls for me!

While I walked home, Uncle Tony would pick Tyra and Monique up from school in the car. He would then take them to the Senior Staff Cafeteria to eat. I, however, was not allowed to eat a meal after school. My uncle would even feel the stove to make sure I had not cooked anything for myself. So, usually, I just snacked on a piece of bread or something that had been left out.

My not being allowed to eat until in the evening would not have been so difficult for me if I had been given lunch money each day or been allowed to take some food with me to school. But I wasn't. While everyone else ate lunch, I'd read a book or take a walk.

I hardly ate one good meal in a day. Understandably so, I began to lose weight. In a short period of time I became very skinny and malnourished.

◆

Upon getting home and eating my bread, I'd do the laundry. It wasn't so bad when we had enough water, but there came a time when I was 15 or 16 years old that we experienced a water shortage at the campus staff quarters. Everyone had to buy water from the truck hawkers to fill their reservoirs, but my uncle refused to do so. He made me fetch water from the stream instead. I did this by carrying the water on my head, in buckets. Every day after school I would make multiple trips until I had filled the three water drums Uncle Tony kept at the house.

The only time I received any help was on the weekends when I had to fill the five hundred gallon water reservoir. Uncle Tony would load his truck with empty 60 gallon containers and drive them to the stream. However, that's where his help ended. He would just sit down and watch while I filled and loaded them back on the truck. Once we got home, I had to single-handedly unload and empty them into the reservoir. Five or six trips later it would be filled to the top, and I would be exhausted..

Often, I would fall asleep at the dining room table. Sometimes, I would make it to bed but did not have the energy to undress. I often slept through the night fully clothed with my shoes still on. I was that tired!

This went on for many years. I had little or no time to study, and I was growing very concerned. Understandably, my grades slipped from As to Cs, Ds, and sometimes Es (equivalent to Fs in the United States). Even still, school continued to be the highlight of my day; it offered a few hours of escape from my dismal life.

Whenever school was over and I set out to go home, just the sight of my uncle's house would cause the tears to flow. I grew increasingly depressed and despondent. I kept saying to myself: *This was not the way my life was supposed to go. How did I end up on this wrong road?*

◆

How I wish my parents would have intervened! However, the truth is that they did not know what was going on. They had no reason to suspect that I would be mistreated by my father's brother, and I had no way of contacting them without my uncle's knowledge. It wasn't as if I could email, text, or use a cell phone to call home.

My uncle successfully kept me away from them. He would visit my parents but never allowed me to go with him. *God only knows what lies he told them.* Each time Uncle Tony returned from Mom and Dad, he would come back with clothes and money that Mom would send me. However, he never gave me any of the presents; he only showed them to me. (To this day I don't know what he did with them.) In the natural I was completely dependent upon him and him alone.

I felt completely on my own, so very alone! I talked to God a lot, asking Him to give me strength and endurance because I wanted to be different than the rest of my family. I wanted to go to university and be able to help my younger siblings, and I knew that would require a good education. I decided that I could and would endure—if for nothing else but a good education.

Above all, though, I wanted the will of God for my life. I firmly believed that God rewards faithfulness and hard work. And I can honestly say that my love for Him deepened as I waited patiently for Him to finish His work in my life.

Isaiah 40:31
But those who hope in the Lord will renew their strength. They will soar on wings like eagles; they will run and not grow weary, they will walk and not faint.

CHAPTER THREE

That I May Know Him

T hrough the years it became obvious to me that the life I was living was no longer mine. It was now God living in me as I learned to yield my life totally to Him. In fact, I developed a hatred for anything that God hates — iniquity, fornication, adultery, gossip, etc. And I was not afraid to challenge those who lived an ungodly lifestyle.

Soon after I had come to live with my uncle, he began dating someone. My cousins and I were told to call her *Aunt Sally.* She was still in college but would come for a visit and stay for days, sometimes weeks. Uncle Tony would drop her off at a bus stop when she was ready to return to campus. This went on for a few years.

One day, after Uncle Tony dropped off *Aunt Sally,* he drove straight to another girlfriend's house. (He had been cheating behind *Aunt Sally's* back even though by that time they were engaged to be married.) Well, my cousins and I were in the car with him when this happened, and I did not like it. I told my uncle to take us (the girls and me) home because it was not godly for him to have a girlfriend after he had committed to marrying *Aunt Sally.*

Uncle Tony would not listen. Not only did he not take us home, he made me pick up a 60 gallon container and fetch some water to fill up his girlfriend's reservoir. At that moment I felt as if he were punishing me for standing up for what I believed in.

I knew that what my uncle was doing was wrong, and I did not want to be a part of it. I felt uneasy even being there; my spirit was not at peace. That evening the woman cooked a meal for all of us, but I refused to eat.

Later that night at about 9:00 PM, while they were drinking and partying, I snuck out and began the one hour walk back to our house, in the dark! When Uncle Tony realized I was not in his girlfriend's house, he began looking for me. I had already walked about five miles when he finally found me. He stopped alongside the road and dragged me into the car.

When we got home, I received the beating of my life – one that I will never forget. I was battered, bruised, and bleeding by the time he finished. In the end I became quite ill from the abuse.

That night, however, was not the first time Uncle Tony had laid his hands on me. I was regularly beaten for being five or ten minutes late from school. Uncle Tony would stand waiting at the door. If I were late, I would be greeted with a heavy slap across my face.

On one occasion I almost lost my life from a severe beating I received from him. It happened when one of his numerous girlfriends came to visit. She had been with us for days when I asked her if she was married. I was shocked when she said, "Yes." I then asked if she had any children. She told me that she had three.

Next, I asked, "Why would you leave your husband and children to come and sleep with my uncle?" She did not answer; she only ran out of the room, crying.

When my uncle came home, the woman told him what had transpired and that she had decided to leave. *Woe to me!* After she left, my uncle *beat the living daylights* out of me.

He told me to mind my own business and that I was too young to tell him what to do.

Often I was led by the Spirit to warn him about certain friends and business partners, but he would only slap me in return. Every time, though, those same friends and business partners would dupe him. He eventually lost everything he had worked so hard for.

◆

Despite everything I endured on a day to day basis, I was never accepted as a "regular girl" at school. Instead, most people assumed I was from a wealthy family and thought I was stuck up (probably because I was never able to socialize). No one knew the turmoil and pain that was my life because I never told anyone.

One particular occasion comes to mind to illustrate this truth. It happened during my final year of high school. A group of us was talking in front of the class when a girl suddenly suggested that we have a competition to see who had the prettiest skin. We all agreed; we stood in a straight line and held out our arms. The "judge" inspected each arm thoroughly and at the end of his inspection, I was recognized as the one with the softest, shiniest, silkiest skin.

However, I was not chosen as winner of the competition. The judge felt it was not fair to the rest of the "less privileged" contestants to choose me. According to him, I was from a wealthy family and therefore able to afford expensive lotions and creams to make my skin look so soft. I was disqualified because my skin's beauty was not *natural*!

This was really surprising to me because I did not use cream. Uncle Tony did not care that I was a young girl needing personal products. Aunt Sally was now married to my uncle and owned a mini-market, but I was never given anything to care for my skin. The only cream I had ever had was that which I had brought from home years earlier, but it was long gone. I had to use cooking oil instead.

Although I knew the truth, although I knew very well that I was anything but privileged, I did not tell them my story. I just couldn't! I did not think they would believe me. So, the discrimination continued.

For example, at the end of every week during morning devotions the teachers would give awards to the outstanding students of the week—the categories included cleanliness and good behavior. Only one student per class could win. Although I was always chosen in my class, the teachers would confer and determine that the award be given to a "less privileged" student. They stated that I was from a wealthy family and that my parents could afford to buy me several uniforms, which enabled me to change uniforms every day. That, of course, was a wrong assumption. The truth was that I only owned two uniforms. I had to wash them by hand and then iron them daily.

I was no way near who they thought I was. I did not enjoy a wealthy lifestyle. Instead, I was made to work very, very hard with no compensation. I was not someone who was so snooty that I refused to spend my *free time* with my schoolmates. Rather, I never knew what it was to enjoy the carefree abandon of youth. (It was a rarity to hear me laugh.) While they considered me privileged, I experienced life in a way most adults could only try to imagine.

Life seemed so unfair to me. I longed for the love and warmth of a family, but my parents lived so far away. The only family I had was Uncle Tony, and he seemed to care less about me. His only acknowledgement of my existence was to make me work like a horse or to beat me senseless whenever I did anything to provoke him.

I had thought that things might change when Uncle Tony married Aunt Sally, but it hadn't. She was not able to help me. As a full-time house wife, Aunt Sally was now dependent on Uncle Tony for everything! She hardly had enough for herself, let alone to share with me.

I had nothing and nobody to comfort me except God. I clung desperately to him, crying to him for help.

"Why is life so unfair?" I queried.

"Why can't anyone see the truth about me?"

"Why won't anyone accept me as a regular girl, not some rich man's child?"

Then, the most amazing thing happened. The Holy Spirit, my Helper, whispered into my ear, "The reason people don't treat you like a 'regular girl' is because you are not a regular girl; you are the daughter of the Most High God, the King of all Kings!" That was all the encouragement I needed.

From that time on I began thinking about how the princesses of this world are held in high esteem and treated with honor, respect, and dignity. They are trained to present themselves in a manner befitting their station. They are groomed to walk, talk, sit, and act a certain way. I began to think of it in this way: *If earthly princesses are treated with such high regard, how much more the daughter of the Most High God?*

My perspective changed. I no longer looked for people to have compassion on me because of the unfairness I suffered in my life. No longer did I see myself as one abandoned and rejected. Instead, I saw a princess—one chosen by God and beloved by Him—when I looked in the mirror. I began to accept the compliments people gave me, realizing that they were actually complimenting the Lord and the work He had done and was doing in my life.

This revelation of who I was opened my eyes to see just how much God really loved me. I was the child of not just any king; I was the favorite daughter of THE KING. Prior to that, I cried constantly. Before I began to understand my true position in Christ, my life had no meaning. In fact, I had often found myself wishing my life would be over, thoughts of suicide occupying my mind.

◆

I remember one particular incident that drove me to the brink of despair. I had just finished high school and had received my examination results. I had made it! I was so proud to have accomplished my goal.

The original agreement with Uncle Tony had been that he would allow me to go to school while I helped him raise his girls and take care of the house. My next step was for me to apply to a university, but that hope was soon dashed. Uncle Tony reneged on his promise; he refused to register me in a university to further my studies. He wanted me to continue as his house maid. On this particular day Uncle Tony had issued the usual threats of beating me if I did not finish all the work on his list and then left for work. *Remember Uncle Tony's original list of chores for me to do?* Well, several years later, I was still being given a chore list daily, one that had become much longer since Aunt Sally gave me things to do as well. For example, I had to wash and maintain clothes for Aunt Sally's new baby.

I wondered where God was. My hopes and dreams seemed to have ebbed away like the tide. I was saddened by my uncle's lack of integrity and hoped against hope that he would change his mind.

Aunt Sally asked me to keep an eye on the shop while she took a nap. I can remember stumbling into the garage (which was her make-shift shop) in a daze. I was tired and weary, but it wasn't merely a physical tiredness; I was mentally exhausted. My life seemed to be spinning out of control, and I just wanted to crawl into a ball and die. At least, then, I thought I would find rest.

When evening came, I had not finished my list of chores. I knew the impending doom that would follow if my uncle were to come home and find that I had not finished my work. So, I snuck out of the house and went deep into the woods to lay down and sleep. I prayed silently that a lion or some other wild animal would find and kill me!

No lions bothered me though. On the contrary, that night I spent in the woods was the best sleep I had experienced in a very long time! I woke up rested. Not even an ant had bitten me, but with the dawn of a new day came the harsh reality of life as it was. I knew I had to go back home and face the music. I had to explain to Uncle Tony where I had been all night long. I shuddered at the thought of the severe beating that awaited me.

To my surprise, though, Uncle Tony did not even question my whereabouts. Even to this day he has never asked me where I was that night. And I now realize it was God's grace that kept me alive all those years in Uncle Tony's house.

Chapter Four

A Ray of Hope

Go d is faithful! He has been with me every step of the way. What's more — I can honestly say that all things, even my most difficult experiences, have worked together for my good.

Romans 8:28 NASB
And we know that God causes all things to work together for good to those who love God, to those who are called according to His purpose.

God's purpose for my life may take me along paths I don't always understand, but I have learned to trust Him. *Why?* Because His plans are always better than my own. He is the Master Planner; He knows just how much I can handle and is always at hand to ensure that I don't drown in the storms of life.

God has consistently sent help through some of the most unlikely of sources. One of them was an aunt of mine who came to visit from London. Aunt Rose was a beautiful woman who was talented, very smart, and highly educated. Most of all, though, I loved her sense of style. My Aunt Rose was the epitome of everything I desired to be in the future.

You may wonder what was so special about Aunt Rose's visit. God used her as a *ray of hope* in my life. She was such a classy lady! Her poise and finesse gave me the determination to strive for my dreams.

God also used a married couple in a profound way in my life. We are close relatives, and I love them very much. They are both highly educated, hard working, and extremely smart. He is a professor. Every visit to their home on the university campus in Ibadan, Oyo State, was a rare treat for me. Whenever I stayed with them and their two beautiful daughters, I would fantasize about having a family of my own that was just as beautiful as theirs. They were totally against my uncle's ill treatment of me, and they were the ones God used to bring about a turning point in my life.

After many conversations and much persuasion they were finally able to convince my uncle to at least secure admission for me at the Polytechnic, which was affiliated with the high school I had attended and where he was a senior staff member. Somewhat reluctantly, he registered me for lectures and introduced me to the lecturers. It was not university, but it was higher learning and would be a step in the right direction.

That night I was unable to sleep...I was just so excited. I couldn't believe what was happening! My dreams finally seemed within reach.

While I was lying there in bed, thinking of how I was finally going to be a Polytechnic student, Aunt Sally and Aunt Rose came into my room. They began teasing me about how it was my 18th birthday and that I still didn't have a boyfriend. They both laughed and said how sad it was that I had missed out on the fun of being a teenager.

My 18th birthday! I had been so excited that I had not even remembered what day it was. Even though there had not been a party for me, it had been a good day, a memorable day. That night I fell asleep with hope in my heart, thinking about all I would accomplish and dreaming about the many friends I would make as a student at the Polytechnic.

◆

I walked to school every day, passing hundreds if not thousands of students on their way to either the Polytechnic or the University. One thing was for sure, I had never been around so many boys, and it was surprising just how many approached me. However, I quickly realized that they did not have the best of intentions.

I received many offers that year, but I did not find it flattering at all. It went something like this: a boy propositioned; I declined. In fact, I was rather annoyed that anyone would think that I was that kind of girl.

People began to call me names. They thought I was just being arrogant and proud since I never said *yes* to them. They did not understand that it had nothing to do with that or them.

Long before I had become a student at the Polytechnic and long before anyone ever flirted with me, I had already made a made a vow of purity to the Lord. I had decided that no one would see my nakedness except the one chosen by God to become my husband. The Holy Spirit had taught me the things of the Kingdom and had shown me reasons why I should not pollute my body, which included fornication. My body was the home, the temple, of the Holy Spirit. As such, it was to be kept pure and holy, a living sacrifice unto God. I asked God to help me keep that vow, and He did.

1 Corinthians 6: 18-20
18 Flee from sexual immorality. All other sins a man commits are outside his body, but he who sins sexually sins against his own body.

19 Do you not know that your body is a temple of the Holy Spirit, who is in you, whom you have received from God? You are not your own;

20 you were bought at a price. Therefore honor God with your body.

◆

I soon became engrossed with my studies. I was very happy because it seemed like I was back on track. Finally, something positive was happening! My life had a semblance of a positive outcome and hope for a great future. However, at the end of the first semester something happened that would shake the very foundation of my faith. It made me question God like never before.

One day the Registrar was making his way from class to class. He was checking the tuition passes of each student. (A tuition pass was a card indicating that a student's tuition had been paid in full; it was given at registration and had to be in the student's possession at the time of inspection. If a student forgot his pass at home, the registrar would consult the records to see if the student's name were listed under the "paid in full" list.) When the registrar came up to me, I had no pass to show him. He checked his list, but to his surprise I was not even registered as a student!

Even as he told me, I was unperturbed. I confidently told the registrar who I was and that my uncle, a senior staff member at the Polytechnic, had registered me. The registrar then invited me to step outside with him for a moment. That's when he informed me that my uncle had never registered me.

This man stood before me and apologized. He confessed that my uncle had made arrangements to allow me to attend classes in order to deceive me into thinking that I was a bona fide student in the school. Uncle Tony had figured my interest and desire for higher education would be fulfilled even if I never got any certificates at the end.

Words cannot accurately describe how I felt at that moment. My whole world came crashing down. There were so many emotions coursing through me. It was as if a dam had broken. I was sad and then angry, but my anger gave way to fear and depression. My head felt so heavy, and my legs were suddenly too weak to hold me up even though my thoughts seemed to be running faster and faster.

This is too heavy – I just can't bear this! What explanation can Uncle Tony give for his atrocious behavior? Why does he hate me so much?.

Somehow, I managed to get home. There, I waited for my uncle to return. I wanted to know why he had done such a thing. His answer, though, turned out to be the straw that broke the proverbial camel's back.

You really don't need an education. After all, if you work hard at growing your Aunt Sally's mini-market and help to make it a more profitable venture, I will give you a portion of the profits as a wedding gift when you get married some day.

I was devastated! It was time for another one-on-one with God. I pleaded my case, asking Him to grant me one request. This time, though, it was not for Him to take my life.

Quite the contrary, I wanted to live. I also wanted to be free. (I remembered how God freed His people Israel from Egyptian bondage.) I asked the Lord to make a way for me to leave my uncle's house. That very night, I decided that I would run away. My head never touched the pillow; instead, I stayed up and talked through my plans with my very best friend...God.

The next step was to share my situation with four of my friends, ones who also lived with relatives but were treated much better than I. Together, we hatched a perfect escape plan. First, they decided to gather some money for me, enough to take me to a neighboring city. Then, once I made it safely there, I would go to my parents. Last, I would enroll in another Polytechnic, one to which I was planning to apply and be accepted on my own merits.

I left Uncle Tony's house without a backward glance. When I did, an incredible sense of peace washed all over me. I knew God was on my side!

Psalms 5:12
For surely, O Lord, you bless the righteous; you surround them with your favor as with a shield.

Psalms 34:17, 19
17 The righteous cry out, and the LORD hears them; he delivers them from all their troubles... 19 A righteous man may have many troubles, but the LORD delivers him from them all

Chapter Five

Jesus, My Connection

To walk back in the door of my parents' home after so many years of bondage—how wonderful it was! Of course our reunion was bittersweet! I had been a little girl when I left home years before, and there I was sitting before them a full grown woman

Finally, though, I was able to recount my ordeal at Uncle Tony's house. My father was livid when he heard how much I had suffered at the hands of his brother. However, he also seemed disappointed with me for not having written a letter or at least finding a way to inform them about what I was going through. I knew then as I know now that my father could not possibly understand the restrictions under which I had lived for so long.

I then told my parents that I had not come to stay. I explained that I was planning to pursue my dream of a college education. Upon hearing this my mother, God bless her, gave me all the money she had saved up over the years. So, after a brief visit I once again left my parents' home for a world unknown. This time I received their blessing as well as finances for the journey.

◆

The Holy Spirit was so very real to me during this time. He truly was my closest companion; I was acutely aware of His presence as I made my way to a city called Ilorin in Kwara State. There, I applied for admission to the Polytechnic and was admitted into the Hotel Management and Catering program.

What a sense of accomplishment I felt that first day! What a great miracle it was to have escaped from my uncle and take the first steps toward my dream. I was truly thankful.

As I went onto campus, I saw three ladies walking toward me. I stopped, introduced myself, and asked if they could direct me to the registrar's office. I explained that I was from a different city and did not know my way around yet. Immediately, I was struck by their willingness to help. They even offered to let me stay with them that evening.

After spending the whole day registering for classes, I went home with my new friends. They told me I could stay with them as long as I wanted or at least until I could find my way around. The most amazing part to me was that they opened their home to me without my having to pay them a penny for my keep! Such hospitality was so very foreign to me after living with my Uncle Tony for all of those years.

That very first evening I found out what made them so different. They were Christians! All three were members of the Fellowship of Christian Students (FCS), an interdenominational group on campus. They asked if I wanted to go with them to their meeting. An emphatic *Yes!* was my answer. What a glorious time I had in the presence of the Lord. We sang, worshipped, and prayed together.

Later, as I was reading my Bible and fellowshipping with God before I fell asleep, I began to thank Him for being there for me. As I did, the Holy Spirit revealed how God had gone ahead of me and prepared the way for me. He had ordered my steps, directing me to three ladies who would take care of as well as introduce me to a fellowship group. Nothing had been by chance; it was all part of God's plan for my life!

It did not take me long to decide that I wanted to permanently stay with my new friends. What a joy it was to live with people who actually liked you and wanted you there. I found a new freedom in my everyday life, knowing that I no longer had to live in fear.

That first FCS meeting I attended was just that, the first of many. I became an active member and even joined the FCS choir. I attended regular meetings as well as various prayer groups, all the while growing in the things of God. Being able to worship together with other believers was such a blessing to me since I had seldom been able to do so during the previous seven years.

◆

With all of my new activities and a full class schedule, the school year seemed to fly. Sooner than I could have imagined, it was almost time for our final exams. For many it was quite emotional since they had reached a crossroads and did not know which way to go next. Everyone was looking for employment, and most began networking in a frenzied effort to "connect" to the best companies.

For me, however, I found how wonderful it is to serve the Lord! I had no "connections" in the natural—I didn't know any highly placed people—but I knew God! Jesus was my connection. Honestly, all I could do was pray; I asked God to not only secure employment for me but for it to be in a five-star hotel.

Through the years, especially those spent in my Uncle Tony's house, I had learned to place my confidence in God. He had taught me how to pray and stay in His presence. Doing so, I knew my life was ordered by Him. He was my

Teacher, my Comforter, and my Confidant. He always led me into His will for my life.

When I got to class one day, there seemed to be some kind of celebration. I asked someone, *Why all the jubilation?* I was told that five students who had been selected to attend a pre-employment screening at The Sheraton in Lagos (a five-star hotel) had just returned. Apparently, the five star hotels throughout Nigeria held pre-employment screenings every year. Their staff would go to all the management universities in the country and select the top five students in each school who would attend. The screening involved rigorous training and a written test at the hotel; those students who passed the written test were employed on the spot.

When I heard this, I asked why no one had told me about it since I was one of the top five in our set. I was informed that I had been passed by because of my Christian faith. Someone had made the decision for me, thinking that I would not like to work in an environment like the Sheraton. I was also told that I had not been selected because I did not have any "connections" or family in Lagos who could provide housing while I was there.

Standing in front of that class, I was so angry. Only later did I realize that I had begun to yell: *I do have a connection in Lagos. I do have family in Lagos. His name is Jesus!* Everyone burst into laughter, not understanding the position that I had as a princess of THE KING.

From that day on they began calling me *Clara Jesus*. The story was told all over campus, and soon it spread to colleges and universities throughout the state. But I didn't care.

I spent that next weekend praying and seeking the face of God. I needed His favor. Then, the following Monday I decided to fast. I was determined to wait upon the Lord for direction. I asked Him to come and take control.

◆

The next thing I did was to make the 200 mile (322 km) journey to Lagos. Once there, I immediately went to the Sheraton Hotel only to find that the gate of the hotel was heavily guarded. There seemed to be no way to gain entry without some form of invitation.

Then, one of the security officers saw me. He called out, *Hey, beautiful girl! What can I do for you?*

I swallowed hard and answered, *I came for the student pre-employment screening.*

Did you receive an invitation in the mail?

No, I didn't.

Then why are you here?

I just heard about the invitation and decided to try out, I explained.

He laughed. Then, he informed me that the testing period was over and that the results had been mailed to the students who had passed. He made it very clear that students could not just show up at the hotel without the school first sending their names to the hotel.

When he finished, however, I politely asked if he would please allow me to see the Human Resource Manager. I thought to myself, *I've come this far, and I'm not leaving without at least trying!*

The security officer waved towards a car that had just driven up, saying *That's him pulling in now. You can wait for him in his office.* (One obstacle overcome!)

As he walked away, I spoke up again, *But I don't know where his office is.* The security guard pointed to an office just a few yards away. Then, he warned me not to tell anyone he had let me in. (Two obstacles overcome!)

When I reached the Human Resource Manager's office, I met with my third obstacle. The manager's secretary told me I could not see him without an appointment. I thought about how far I had come and how I had boasted about my God.

Again, I knew I just couldn't leave without trying. I sat there in the lobby, waiting for a miracle.

After what seemed like a very long time the secretary walked through the lobby where I was sitting. When she saw me, she expressed her concern about my still being there. I took that opportunity to plead with her. I asked if she would allow me to see the HR Manager for just a few minutes. Right then and there she promised to try even though she did not think he would want to see me.

A few minutes later, though, she came back. *You are very lucky,* she said with a smile on her face. *He wants to see you.* She then ushered me into the manager's office and left. (Three obstacles overcome!)

When I walked into the office, I went down on my knees before the manager. (This is a sign of humility and respect within the Nigerian culture.) He told me to get up and sit in a chair. He then asked, *Now, tell me why you refused to leave when you were informed that you needed an appointment to see me?*

That's all I needed. I quickly launched into my story, telling him about the hardships I had faced and my determination to succeed in life. I explained that my experiences had given me resilience and fortitude. I assured him that I was very hard working and that he must look beyond my slender, somewhat fragile looking frame. I begged for an opportunity to prove this to him and promised that if given the chance, I would not disappoint him.

The HR manager just looked at me for a long time. Finally, he spoke: *Even if I said okay, I am not sure there are any more vacancies. And if there are vacancies, you must pass the pre-employment screening test first before you are considered.* (Fourth obstacle overcome!)

Okay, sir! was my quick response.

He sent for the Training Manager. When she arrived in his office, he asked her if any department in the hotel had posted a vacancy. It turned out that the chef needed assistance in the kitchen.

The HR manager turned to me and asked, *Can you work in the kitchen, Clara?*

Yes, sir!

Alright, then. Go with the training manager for your test, and good luck.

(Fifth obstacle overcome!)

Once inside the training room, I found two guys sitting there. After introductions were made, I realized they were from one of the best universities in Nigeria. They had been invited for pre-screening for the same kitchen position.

The Training Manager handed the test to us. It was a one hundred question, multiple choice exam. She told us that we had twenty minutes to finish, set the alarm, and then left the room.

I used the first five minutes to pray: *God, even if I knew the answers to these questions, 20 minutes is not enough time for me to finish the test. O Lord, you have brought me this far. Please do not disappoint me.*

Then, I lifted up my pen toward heaven and continued praying: *Holy Spirit, come and take control because I don't know the answers to these questions.*

With that I began working on the test. Since it was multiple choice, all I had to do was shade the correct answer. So, I began choosing what seemed most accurate to me. Just as I thought, the alarm went off before I could finish. I had only made it to question #65.

The examiner came in and collected our papers. Next, she told us to wait while our tests were graded electronically. I sat there thinking, *If only I could have finished the entire test, then I probably would have a fighting chance to get a good grade.*

Looking at the facts alone, I would have had to admit that my chances were looking grim, but I refused to consider failure. Instead, I sat there silently praying. My mind turned to a familiar scripture, one that over the years had brought me peace during the harshest of trials:

<u>Psalm 121:1-8 NIV</u>
I lift up my eyes to the hills — where does my help come from? My help comes from the Lord, the Maker of heaven and earth. He will not let your foot slip — he who watches over you will not slumber; indeed, he who watches over Israel will neither slumber nor sleep. The LORD watches over you the LORD is your shade at your right hand; the sun will not harm you by day, nor the moon by night. The LORD will keep you from all harm he will watch over your life; the LORD will watch over your coming and going both now and forevermore.

My help comes from the Lord, I reminded myself softly. *He brought me this far; He will finish the good work he has begun in me. God watches over me and if anyone out of the three of us will pass this test, it will be me! I have never heard that God has ever forsaken a righteous person, and He will not start with me"*

As I continued to pray, my confidence level soared as scripture after scripture kept running through my heart and mind, filling me with assurance:

Philippians 1:6
Being confident of this, that he who began a good work in you will carry it on to completion until the day of Christ Jesus.

Psalm 37:25
I was young and now I am old, yet I have never seen the righteous forsaken; or their children begging bread.

After what seemed like an *eternity*, the Human Resource Manager finally returned with the results. He explained that in order to pass the test, you must have at least 50 correct answers. He turned to the two guys that took the test along with me and told them he was sorry but that they had failed the test. He then looked at me and said, *"Well, well, Clara. You scored 51. You passed the test. Congratulations! Now go to the Training Manager's office for further instructions and obtain an orientation schedule.* (Sixth obstacle overcome!)

I shook hands with my former opponents and left. I felt like singing out loud: *For this God is my God, for ever and ever, He will be our guide, even to the end (Psalm 48:14).* Tears ran down my cheeks as I thought about God's goodness to me. All I could say was *God, you did it again!*

Upon my return to school I told my course mates what the Lord had done for me. Some did not believe my story. Others said that they found it difficult to even imagine what I was telling them. But one in particular stated, *Clara truly had Jesus in Lagos.*

A few weeks later the school year was over, and it was time to begin work at the Sheraton. Out of the top five students that were pre-screened for employment by the hotel management, only one of them (besides me, of course) had been selected. Cynthia received her confirmation of appointment through the mail, so the two of us left together to fill our new positions.

Life seemed to be wide open and full of possibilities. Without doubt I knew that the Lord Himself had enabled me to overcome every obstacle in my way. He had truly proven to me that He alone was the only "connection" I needed. I could not wait to see what He was going to do on my behalf when I reached Lagos!

Chapter Six

Highs and Lows

In life I have found that a great accomplishment (a "high") is often followed by difficulty and hardship (a "low"). *Why does this seem to be the case?* Some might say that it is just the way life works. But I would say that your enemy wants to discourage you, get you off track, and cause you to turn around and go the opposite direction.

I experienced quite a "high" when I received my certificate from the Polytechnic as well as a sought-after position with a five-star hotel. I had accomplished my goal, and my parents were very proud of me. I had done what I said I would do. In fact, I had done better than they had even thought I would or could. That was a great feeling!

Then came the first low. I had to move and get settled before reporting for orientation at the Sheraton. My mother had given me the address of my brother who lived in Lagos, so at least I knew I would have a place to stay until I could find my own. He was expecting me.

Having already said goodbye to my friends, I set out very early one morning. I arrived at the Lagos Ojota transit station by 10 AM. Then, since I only had my brother's address and no directions, I began asking questions of the people around me. Unfortunately, those I asked really did not know where I was going but directed me anyway. I went north, south, east, and west...all in an attempt to find my brother. I was starting to run out of cash, and I did not know what to do.

Finally, at 3 PM a good Samaritan came my way who not only could give me accurate directions to where I was going but had lived in that very community at one time. He even knew the location of my brother's office, which he said was close to the bus stop. However, he told me that my final destination was all the way on the other side of the city

After another three hours of waiting in line and riding even more buses, I found my brother's office. (I am not sure what I would have done if he had not been working late that evening.) I was so happy to see him! I had made it; I was in Lagos; my hopes and dreams were within reach.

Orientation was the first thing that both Cynthia and I had to do as new employees of the Sheraton. The schedule was rigorous, but every day I adjusted a little more to my new surroundings. I became more and more familiar with the hotel, the staff, and what would be expected of me.

I knew there would be lots of hard work ahead. That, however, did not concern me. I was used to that. However, I did have lots of questions, questions I only asked of the Lord when I would lay down each evening before I slept.

Once orientation was completed I began my work in the Main Kitchen as a prep cook. What an eye opening experience that was! I discovered I was working in a very ungodly atmosphere, one in which the employees talked more trash than I had ever heard in my life. A steady stream of curse words and course jokes were the usual fare each and every day.

The kitchen staff especially enjoyed mocking each other and all who dared walk into their domain. The servers were picked on the most! I felt sorry for them because I knew what it was like, having lived through that kind of treatment when I lived in my uncle's house. So, I never laughed at the staff jokes. However, my non-participation quickly set me a part from everyone else, and it wasn't long before everyone knew that I was a born-again Christian.

Then, all attention turned on me. The staff began to call me names and openly ridicule me. I became the butt of their jokes.

Furthermore, the members of the kitchen staff insisted that it would not be very long before I would change. All of them were convinced that I was a fake. They had seen other people come to the hotel as professing Christians only to watch them change the longer they stayed on staff.

According to those who taunted me the women they were discussing had been Christians (at least by their outward appearance). They had covered their hair and worn long sleeves and skirts or outdated dresses. I heard how those employees had been known to carry their Bibles around with them but were now the most flirtatious. I was told that they had compromised by going out with managers and even the hotel guests.

Words, words, words. They came my way every day. I was given such a hard time; it was very difficult to keep my attention on the work in front of me.

My co-workers even went so far as to tell me that I was too beautiful to be in the kitchen. Then, I found out that they were all betting when management would move me to the front desk in order for me to be seen by the guests. Less than six months...that was the wager.

What's more, everyone in the kitchen thought I would receive lots of tips from the hotel guests if I were trans-ferred. They firmly believed that the money would cause me to compromise my faith just like many other employees had done before me. However, they did not know me very well. I was not about to change!

<u>**1 Peter 5:8-11**</u>
Be self-controlled and alert. Your enemy the devil prowls around like a roaring lion looking for someone to devour. Resist him, standing firm in faith, because you know that your brothers in throughout the world are under going the same kind of sufferings.

Every day the same group would gather. They even called in some witnesses to confirm what they were saying was true. Then, one day in particular I stood up to them and in the power of the Holy Spirit told them:

I am not disputing the fact that many have said they were Christians, only to backslide when tempted. But I am not one of them! It is possible to be a born-again Christian and stand in the gap for God while working in this hotel. You will have to change what you say! You will have to say that there was at least one who did not change, one who did not yield to any form of deception.

When I finished, I ran to the locker room. I just had to have some time with the Lord. I asked Him to please back me up, to confirm my words. I reminded Him that I always bragged on Him and His ability. I admitted that I did not know what I was going to face but that I wanted to hold on to my confession of His grace. Then, with peace in my heart I went back to work...praising Him as I did.

<u>**Esther 4:1**</u>
For if you remain silent at this time, relief and deliverance for the Jews will arise from another place, but you and your father's family will perish.

And who knows but that you have come to royal position for such a time as this?

Sheraton Lagos staff member 1990

During this time I experienced the Lord's protection in a very special way. As I have already said, I was living with one of my brothers and his wife until I could find my own place. And although he lived in Lagos, his home was very far away from the Sheraton. (With Lagos being a city of 10 million people you can *live* in Lagos and still be an hour or more away from another destination in the city.) The distance I had to travel made for a very long work day!

While making the journey to work one day, I had a frightening experience. I hailed a cab. The driver already had two passengers, but that did not seem strange to me since multiple people often shared the same cab because it cut down on the cost.

I sat in the back seat with one of the original two passengers because the other person was already sitting in front with the driver. Almost immediately they started asking me questions. I did not mind. In fact, I did not even think anything was wrong until the driver would not stop at the Sheraton as I requested. He just passed by the entrance to the hotel without slowing down.

I became very scared and began to plead with him, trying to make him understand that I would lose my job if I were late. He kept driving. Then, I realized that the other two passengers must be working with the driver when they became hostile towards me. I knew I was in trouble.

We drove around and around the city streets for more than an hour. All the while, the three kept asking me if I had a bank account and if I had any money at home. I explained over and over that I had just given all of my money to my mother, who had come for a visit and had left that very morning.

I've only been living in Lagos for just a few weeks. I've only been paid twice. I have no extra money; I have no savings.

Thankfully, my kidnappers believed me. However, they still demanded my purse. They wanted all of the money I had with me at the time.

To be honest, I was not sure what would happen next. I really thought they might physically harm me so when they suddenly slowed down and pushed me out the door, I was so very thankful. To this day I am not sure why they chose to let me go. However, there is one thing of which I am very sure — the Lord's angels were protecting me that day.

After the initial shock of hitting the road, I tried to stand up and move to the side of the street. I certainly did not want another car to come by and hit me while I was lying there in the dirt. Although I could already see bruises forming on my legs and hands, I was able to push myself up to a standing position and then made my way to safety.

A few people were standing nearby. I quickly told them my story, which they believed because they had seen me thrown from the car. They were very kind, even offering me money so that I could get to work.

By the time I got to work I was two hours late. When I explained what had happened to me, my manager felt sorry for me. He excused my tardiness.

Later that day, a fellow employee rejoiced with me. We both knew that I could have been held for ransom, raped, or killed. To God be the glory! Surely the Lord had been watching over me. That my kidnappers even slowed down to let me out after they were convinced that I didn't have any money was a miracle.

When the news of my kidnapping got around work, a few employees offered to be my roommate. Cynthia was one of them and although I had not really known her at school, she seemed very nice. She told me that she had just sub-let one room with a joint kitchen and bathroom. Since hers was the closest to work, I agreed; we would share the rent.

The next morning Cynthia took me to my new home. On the way there I saw a church, Latter Rain Ministries. Then and there, I decided to visit once I had gotten settled into my new home. Little did I know then that God had already prepared a spiritual father whom He would use to teach and preach the undiluted word of God, someone who would help me fulfill my destiny at Sheraton Lagos. *How?* For, it would be through Pastor Bakare's leadership and my involvement at Latter Rain that the Lord answered my prayer—that I would be one born-again Christian employee at the Sheraton who would not backslide under any circumstances.

In less than six months—exactly what the kitchen staff predicted—I was transferred to the front office. However, when I first heard the news that I would become a receptionist, I was unhappy. I remembered what everyone had said about the temptations I would face in such a position and thought the kitchen (out of sight of the guests) would be best for me. So, I requested a meeting with the executive chef. I thought he might be willing to change the Management's mind if I told him how I loved to work in the kitchen.

We met, but told me that there was nothing he could do to help: *Management's decision is final. They think you are wasted in the kitchen. They feel you would be more profitable to the Sheraton if you were in the front office..*

I walked away from our meeting both sad and scared. Immediately, I began to pray for God to help me. I knew I would need the comfort of the Holy Spirit if I were going to make it.

My training in front of the house began in the business center. From there I went to the switchboard. I was then moved to the reservation desk and then on to the reception desk.

During the time I spent as a telephone operator some guests began to request to see me at the front desk because my voice was very different on the phone. They wanted to meet the person whose voice they were hearing. So, I would be called out to meet the guest. From that point on I began receiving tips.

I was handling the pressure well and actually enjoying my job when another test came why. I was moved to the position of receptionist at The Club within the Sheraton. I quickly found out that there was quite a rivalry among the two groups of staff even though we really all worked at the same hotel. It did not take long before I became the subject of employee discussions once again. Some even accused me of wrongdoing.

I will have to admit that the atmosphere at the club was not the best, but that did not mean I was going to change. Of course, the club was not open during the day, so that added to its reputation. Its hours were from 5:00 PM to 4:30 AM. A DJ was always on duty, and the dance floor was usually full.` Wealthy clients brought their wives and business associates as well as dates (including call girls). Cigarette and cigar smoke filled the aired. Some guests would drink too much, their behavior becoming outrageous.

My testimony, though, is that I became the influencer, not the influenced. I made friends with my fellow co-workers, and they knew where I stood on certain subjects. I am very proud to be able to say that most of them got born again while I was on staff and others have since made a decision for Christ.

◆

The grace of God and the powerful fear of God kept me walking for the Lord. I was encouraged to stay the course each week as I listened to and applied messages from great men of God like Pastor Bakare. The Word of God became my sustenance through those days of working in the club at the Sheraton. So much so that not only can I say that I stood in the gap for God and did not compromise my standards but I also grew stronger and stronger in the Lord and in my faith.

One particular message I still remember; it challenged me. Pastor Bakare told about a certain family. The husband had traveled out of town. One evening around midnight their child became sick to the point of death. I remember the pastor saying that it would take a woman who had a personal relationship with God to stay calm and lay hands on the child and pray, it would take a woman of faith to authoritatively bind and cast out the spirit of death even before the doctor or the pastor were able to arrive. Pastor also applied the same principal to business owners and individuals when it came to having our personal requests answered by God. I decided that day that I wanted to be that kind of wife, mother, business owner, and woman.

Pastor Bakare also made it clear to everyone that our relationship with God can not be attained or reached without accepting the work and sacrifice of Jesus Christ. He insisted that we must each recognize and rely up Christ's blood alone for our salvation. As I sat in service each week I learned how my journey to holiness began the day that I believed in my heart and confessed with my mouth that Jesus Christ is the Son of God, the One who died for my sins, rose again the third day, and now sits at the right hand of the Father. His blood was the atonement for all of humanity's sin, once and for all, washing me clean and paving the way for me to become the daughter of the Most High God.

Romans 10:9
That if you confess with your mouth, "Jesus is Lord," and believe in your heart that God raised him from the dead, you will be saved.

Sitting under the teachings of this anointed man of God, I also became more and more aware of the enemy's devices. I realized that the devil would like nothing more than for me to fall into sin. My testimony was at stake! That is why I chose to not have a boyfriend while I worked at the club. (I would not even go out with a man, any man, during that time.) And honestly, my decision helped to keep me holy in an unholy environment.

Day after day and month after month I grew more and more in the things of the Lord. My desire to serve and know him increased. I wanted to learn how to hear God's voice, know His will, and discern the truth each and every day. Colossians, Chapter One, became my prayer. I wanted to know Him in such a way that I would remain strong no matter what I faced in life and that I would obtain all of the promises of God.

Colossians 1:9-12
For this reason, since we heard about you, we have not stop praying for you and asking God to fill you with knowledge of his will through all spiritual wisdom and understanding. And we pray this in order that you may live a life worthy of the Lord and may please him in every way: bearing fruit in every good work growing in the knowledge of God, being strengthened with all power according to his glorious might so that you may have great endurance and patience, and joyfully giving thanks to the father, who had qualified you to share in the inheritance of the saint in the kingdom of light.

◆

One year passed. I could not believe it. So much had happened to me since I had had my *Jesus* Connection in Lagos. I had been through a series of highs and lows, but I was still coming out on top. For me, life was better than ever.

Chapter Seven

Doubts, Temptations, and Triumphs

Life was good and getting better all of the time. I really liked my job, loved my church, and could not wait to see what was next for me. In such a short period of time I had gone from being a servant in my uncle's home to graduating from technical college at the top of my class, to garnering a job at one of the nation's finest hotels, to beginning the climb up the corporate ladder.

Then, I heard that the Sheraton would be renovating a portion of the hotel. There was even to be a name change: The Sheraton Hotel and Towers. The standard of the tower section was to be much higher than the rest. It was being designed to accommodate the needs and desires of presidents, governors, and very important guests. An announcement was made that there would be a special selection process for the employees who would be assigned to the Towers. We were told that anyone on the current staff who felt qualified could apply. Immediately, I decided if anyone was going to get a job there, it would be me.

As the day for interviews got closer, a great panic arose among the staff. Jealousy and desperation ran rampant. Some were willing to do anything to be selected. I just continued to stand and believe.

The pre-selection list was posted. My name was on it. However, people then began telling me that I was not qualified and would not be chosen in the end. They suggested I not even show up for the final interview, giving me several reasons why it was impossible for me to be chosen. Unfortunately, I began to believe them; I began to doubt myself and my God.

You have no experience! You have only been in the hotel business for a year.

I forgot the fact that I held a degree in hotel management and had been in the top five of my class. I also forgot the many promotions I had received since I had arrived at The Sheraton.

You don't wear makeup.

Their comments made me very unsure of myself. I fell back into old thought patterns and feelings, forgetting that I was God's princess and beautiful in His sight.

Your hair is not right. (My hair was very long and still natural. I had never used a relaxer or perm.)

I also forgot that God looks at the heart while people look at the outward appearance.

Some simply said, *And you call yourself a Christian.*

I began to doubt my ability to be salt and light no matter where God places me. I forgot that I was to be His ambassador.

I decided not to show up for the final interview. However, I was scheduled for work that day; my shift at the club was to begin at 5:00 PM. I just hoped that all of the interviews would be finished by the time I got there. Quite honestly, I did not want to hear any more about it.

But that was not to be! For, as soon as I stepped into the hotel and began walking toward the employee time clock, I heard somebody call my name. It was one of the judges from the interview panel. They had been deliberating all day and could not come to an agreement. I later found out that they had sent for me but since I did not have a cell phone, they had been unable to reach me.

Clara, come here.

So, I went to the office. There were about five managers sitting there.

Did you not sign up for the towers interview?

Yes, I did.

Why didn't you show up?

I thought I was not qualified.

Are you still interested?

Yes, Sir.

Are you ready for the interview now?

Yes, Sir.

I did the interview. I thought it was fair. The next day the results were posted. I had passed! But that was just the beginning.

Later, I was called back to a conference room where the managers were holding a meeting. The Human Resources manager who had been absent at the final decision of my being chosen was greatly concerned about my Holiness Christianity lifestyle. He believed the hotel was for business. He especially emphasized the need for the new Towers' staff to smart, individuals who would wear the latest make-up and have nice up-to-date hairstyles. He went on to say that he had known me for over a year and believed beyond a doubt that I would never wear make-up or relax my hair.

Standing in front of everyone, I was told that the only way I would win one of the coveted new positions is if I would start using make-up and be ready to perm my hair. I was also told that I would be sent to grooming and behavioral training classes. The only reason, they said, that I was being given this opportunity was that I was qualified in every other expectation and quality needed. I was then given 20 minutes to think about their offer and come back with my decision.

I left the room and headed straight for the employee locker room. Once there, I began to ask the other lady staff members who were Christians for their opinions and advice. There was a distinct division among the born-again ladies. Some believed I should not take the promotion; others believed I should go back and take the job right away. The second group told me that make-up or permed hair does not qualify or disqualify you from heaven because it is with your heart you believe and with your mouth confess that Jesus is Lord. These same ladies brought out make-up and made me up right there and then. It was a first for me.

Romans 10:10
For it is with your heart that you believe and are justified, and it is with your mouth that you confess and are saved.

When I went back to the conference room, where the managers were waiting, with make- up on my face and a promise to perm my hair, everyone seemed happy and excited for me. All except for the human resources manager! He demanded that I report to him every day, saying "I will only believe this is real if you keep your promise for three weeks."

Upon hearing that I had been accepted (with conditions) I made my way back to the staff locker room. Everyone was waiting to hear my news. I explained what I would have to do to keep the job, and to my surprise each one of them went to their bags and began to give me whatever make-up they had with them that day. Then, the rest of the week I received so many gifts that I did not have to spend any of my money to buy cosmetics for the next year or two.

The greatest part of the whole make-up or no make-up as a believer was that when I got to church that Sunday morning my Pastor was preaching about what was acceptable attire as a Christian. He did not know what I was going through. He did not know that I was about to make a decision that would change my life forever. What a confirmation to me that message was!

Pastor Tunde Bakare discussed many things that day. He mentioned that wearing trousers (pants) by a woman, weaving one's hair, or even dressing in sport clothes and sneakers (tennis shoes) does not exempt someone from being a believer or stop anyone from coming to church. He said, "You can come to church just the way you are." What a gift I was given that day; what freedom I received!

◆

The Sheraton Tower staff, me included, began to prepare immediately for our new positions. Training and grooming classes were given in order to educate us how to respond to the various guests that would be lodging in The Towers. We studied how to serve the likes of kings, queens, presidents, Governors and other VIPs. The Sheraton was expecting an international clientele, not just Africans. Therefore, we had to be coached in the behavior and body language of many nationalities, not just those from the continent of Africa. This included the use of cosmetics and fragrances.

After hours and hours of preparation The Towers finally opened. I was so very excited; I could not wait to get started. However, there was no way for me to know that my wonderful opportunity to advance would be accompanied by the greatest temptations I had ever experienced or imagined.

I, having grown up with so little while desiring so much more, was now surrounded by untold wealth. However, I saw not only the advantages that riches and prestige offered but also the temptations that can accompany them. For example, fornication and adultery were every day events. I know this because I became the person who was asked to pass messages and information from visitors to my guests in the hotel. I watched women (married and not) go with men because of who they were, what they owned, and how much they could and would offer in return for an evening, a weekend, or sometimes longer. I even saw students from various universities abandon their lectures in order to lodge with a guest or travel out of town with the rich men who frequented our hotel.

I remember one student in particular. Although she dated a very wealthy man throughout her entire school days, one who often stayed in our hotel, she became engaged to another. At that time she introduced the rich man to her fiancé. She described him as a God-send, someone who had helped her with her financial needs. He, of course, was very grateful, not knowing what had really taken place between his future bride and the man who would become the chairman of their wedding. (The girl's family knew the truth but denied it.) The man even bought a brand new car for the new couple as a gift.

It looked as if there were no consequences to the rampant sin I saw played out in front of me every time I went to work. It looked as if it might be okay to let someone take care of me for a change. It looked as if it might be beneficial to me and my future to do the same. However, I was determined not to take the same path.

That did not mean, however, that I was not tempted. I had men who promised me heaven on earth if I would only go out with them. Some of the promises included: a house, a car, enough money to quit my job and do business, marriage, a modeling contract overseas, and lots more.

One guy in particular tested me. He gave a lot of money to everybody but me. He said that he would only give me money (more than I could ever imagine) if I would just give him something to make him feel special. For example, he might ask me to cut a leaf from a flower on the table or bring him something to him.

My answer was always *NO!* Even my friends pled and urged me to give him something so that he would be satisfied. I continued to say, *NO!* I knew there was more to it than his seemingly simple requests.

This went on for quite some time. The man in question was furious when he found out that I had gotten married. He even threatened to destroy my marriage so that I could come back and marry him. My answer: *...only if God makes mistakes. And I know God does not make mistakes. My marriage is final.*

However, let me make one thing very clear. If it had not been for God, I do not know what I would have done, what decisions I would have made. In fact, without my growing relationship with Jesus and my daily being led and guided by the Holy Spirit I am convinced that I would not be writing this testimony today. God was on my side; He upheld me and protected me right in the middle of a very sinful and potentially dangerous situation.

Psalm 124:1-8

If the Lord had not been on our side—let Israel say — if the Lord had not been on our side when men attacked us, when their anger flared against us, they would have swallowed us alive; the flood would have engulfed us, the torrent would have swept over us, the raging waters would have swept us away.

Praise be to the Lord, who has not let us be turn by their teeth. We have escaped like a bird out of the fowler's snare; the snare has been broken and we have escaped. Our help is in the name of the Lord, the Maker of heaven and the earth.

Chapter Eight

God's Reward

Many the proverb I learned from my parents. However, the ones I remember the most are those I myself have proven to be true in my own life. They cease to be just wise sayings passed down from one generation to another, they become truth.

Proverbs 13:21
Misfortune pursues the sinner, but prosperity is the reward of the righteous.

How do I know this is true? I experienced it firsthand while working at The Towers. God has a way of rewarding His own people, those who are in right-standing with Him.

I want you to know that I was richer than any staff member that ever worked in The Towers with me. The reason is not because I took money for favors or because I became someone's friend to get ahead. *No!* I contended with God, and the fruit of the Kingdom of God was my reward.

Guests often gave me presents and monetary gifts. I believe these blessings were sent by God to reward my righteousness. The sealed envelopes were my favorite things to open because I would often find thousands of US Dollars or British Pounds stuffed inside.

◆

Thankfully, my biological father had taught me how to multiply money when I was just a small girl. Those lessons became the foundation for the financial decisions I made during this time. My father had taught me to always have two different bank accounts. One was solely to be used to save money for business purposes. He explained it this way: if you earn 500, you tell the bank to automatically direct 400 to this (business) account. Place the remaining 100 in your checking account—that is what you spend rain or shine for gifts, clothing, food, etc. The other 400 you save until there is a business opportunity that will yield a return.

What wisdom my Father had shared with me! He may not have received a formal education, but he knew the principle of multiplication. He also knew how to share that wisdom with me, giving me the tools and the knowledge I needed to build and accumulate wealth. wealth. He trained me well! Even to this day, whenever God allows any money to come into my hand, the first thing that comes to my mind is *how can I multiply it?*

Although I had not lived in my father's home since I was a young girl, I continued to hear the lessons he had taught me. Also, every week I sat in church and listened to my spiritual father teach lessons on the spiritual side of God's blessing, stewardship, abundance, leadership, and wealth management. Where I had seen my natural father neglect the Lord, the Church, and his family in his pursuit of wealth, I saw my spiritual father teaching and doing the opposite. I saw a new and better standard raised in front of me:

Matthew 6:33
But seek first His kingdom and his righteousness,
and all these things will be given to you as well.

Dr. Bakare encouraged each of us to pursue the Lord first. He preached the uncompromised good news of the Kingdom of God, challenging us to apply God's Word to our personal lives as well as our business endeavors. We were then called upon to take what we had been given to the nations.

In addition, I had two mothers after whom I could pattern myself. Both my biological mother and my spiritual mother, Mrs. Bamidele Bakare, had a motherly heart filled with a great love and concern for their family as well as others who came their way. Both were women who had humble spirits, loving the Lord greatly. What lessons they too had taught me!

◆

I saved for over a year. When I thought it was time, I started planning the opening of my business. I had already been purchasing equipment that I would need from the time that I was in school and had been adding to my stock every chance I got. I kept it all in one room in my rented, one bedroom house. It sure was crowded in there, what with an industrial mixer and oven along with my other treasured inventory.

My plan was to open a bakery and coffee shop. I would not only sell snacks and coffee but would also offer catering services. It would be an upper class establishment, one that would be able to provide excellent service for weddings, special programs, and other large gatherings. I wanted to be "the" place to come.

I was very excited about my dream coming to pass. I paid a deposit of about 50,000 Naira, which would have been the equivalent of approximately $1800 US at the time, for the shop I wanted to rent while it was still under construction. I had even done all of the paperwork and gotten approved for 100 crates of soft drinks from the Coca-Cola headquarters.

◆

This dream was more than just my wanting to succeed, more than my wanting to be a successful business woman. I wanted to be married. And having realized that it would not be possible for me to be a wife (and mother) while I was working day and night at the hotel, I thought that if I started my business then I would always be around for my family.

My prayer had been that God would direct me toward the man he had planned to be my husband. And I did not believe for just any man. No! I knew that God had kept me for the man who had found favor with Him, one I could love, cherish, and respect. So, I added this "unknown" man to my prayer list and instead of praying for a husband, I was praying for the man who was to be my husband. A big difference between the two!

One thing I did know. If ever I needed God in my life, now was the time. I needed Him to intervene on my behalf because I realized that I did not fully understand how to rightly measure the man for me. Marriage is a once in a life-time decision, and I did not want to be led astray. I had seen so much at The Sheraton; I did not want to fall for the same type of traps that I had seen laid for the women I had met and watched while working.

From what I could see by watching others, relationships either drew you closer to God or pulled you away from Him. I, for one, wanted to insure that I continued my relationship with Him. I did not want any man to lead me astray from the love of God.

God is always ahead of every situation in human life. To prove my point it was at the very time I began praying about my husband that Pastor Bakare started teaching a series on marriage. He showed us from the Word of God that Christians should not be unequally yoked with an unbeliever, saying something life "birds of the same feather flock together". As you can well imagine, I did not miss a service.

◆

I can't explain it, but the moment I started praying for my husband a lot of men started showing up. Some that were Christians told me that they had seen a vision and that I was to be their wife. (Well, I knew that could not be true. I could not be a wife to all of them!) There were even some outside the Body of Christ who asked me to marry them. (And that was not going to happen!)

I remember one man in particular. He was one of the ones who told me that he had had a vision of us marrying. He started showing up at my work. He would offer to walk me home from church. I finally had had enough and said, "Marriage would mean my spending the rest of my life together with you. As it is, it's hard for me to spend five minutes with you. That is torture already, so I can just imagine the rest of my life with you." I was sorry to have to do it, but he was not accepting "No!" as my answer.

Another of the Christian men who told me that it was God's will for us to marry also found out that I could be blunt when forced. I informed him, "I will be praying because God is not an author of confusion. If God revealed to you that I am to be your wife, He will speak to me also." I was willing to wait. I wanted to make sure that I had peace about accepting his offer of marriage.

As it happened, the two of us were invited to attend a local wedding. Well, at the reception he offered to introduce me to his family as his fiancée. I answered, saying "I don't think that would be a good idea since we are still waiting on God." He became furious and started to yell at me in front of everybody. Then, he began to curse me out. Although it was uncomfortable and very embarrassing, I had my answer. I would not be accepting his marriage proposal because I knew the Word of God was very clear about not associating with someone who has a temper. He was not the man for me.

> **Proverbs 22:24-25**
> **Do not make friends with a hot-tempered man, do not associate with one easily angered, or you may learn his ways and get yourself ensnared.**

> **<u>Proverbs 29:22</u>**
> **An angry man stirs up dissension, and a hot-tempered one commits many sins.**

There were so many more until my man, God's favored one, finally showed up. And I will tell you that he did not come with roses, riches, or gifts of diamonds and pearls. In fact, when I met him, he did not look as if he held much promise of being the one who would eventually become my husband. In the natural the future held nothing between us, but he was the one that the Lord God Almighty, the creator of heaven and earth, has set aside for me, his daughter.

◆

My future husband was a long time, active member of the same church I attended, Latter Rain Ministries. However, we only became aware of each other after a dear brother in Christ, who was very active at my house fellowship, introduced him: "Clara, this is Paul, my uncle who previously lived in the United States of America. He will now be attending our house fellowship." Nothing earth shattering took place, no voice from heaven was heard—just a simple introduction.

Weeks rolled into months. Paul and I began to talk. After some time our friendship grew stronger as we began to find out that we both had a few things in common. But the fact that he was trying to relocate to the United States stood in the way because I had a lot of prospects and a promising future in Nigeria, not America. I was about to start a generational business and was sure of becoming a millionaire very soon. Why would I want to become involved with someone who was planning to emigrate?

At the time Paul had never been invited to my house. I had a rule: only sisters could visit. It was another safeguard I had in place. However, one fateful day after the church service I showed him where I lived. He came in but went no farther than the living room.

Our Pastor did not support Christian men being seen in a Christian woman's room, encouraging everyone to avoid the very appearance of evil. So, my landlady stood in the place of my mother that day and acted as a chaperone. We sat in her living room, and she offered Paul and others who were there a Coca-Cola.

Paul has told me that he will never forget that first visit. *Why*, you ask? My landlady took the offered Coca-Cola from a crate by the wall, not the refrigerator. My husband says that he will never forget how hot that Coke was. He knew he had to earn her approval that day, so he drank half of the Coke just to please her. It was only because of me, he says.

After some time went by Paul extended an invitation for me to come to his house. We, of course, were not the only ones there. Actually, there was a large group of us. And it was only after my visit that our relationship became a bit serious.

Then, one day, Paul sent his younger brother to call on me. (This is according to Nigerian custom.) That was the day Paul asked me if I would marry him. I was very shocked; we had become close friends and even prayer partners, but I had not been thinking about him in that way.

It was true that we had talked a lot about life and the future. We had even discussed our desire to be married, what type of home we each wanted, how many children, and so on. From the discussions we had I already knew that he genuinely loved the Lord, was a highly learned Bible scholar, and was very intelligent. However, I did not give him an answer immediately. Instead, I told him that I would go and pray about it. I said that I wanted to wait on God concerning a few questions I had.

The main question I had was rooted in the fact that Paul wanted me to relocate to America with him. I could not understand why God would want me to marry someone who wanted to live in America when I was doing so well in Nigeria, especially for my age. I had accumulated so much through the help and leadership of the Holy Spirit. I believed I was on track to become a millionaire in Nigeria, which would afford me so many luxuries. I knew I would have the money to vacation abroad whenever I pleased. But live somewhere else other than my own nation? No, I just could not do it.

My answer, then, was this: "I'll marry you on one condition. Promise me you will never relocate to America."

Now it was my turn to wait. Paul loved America, a country in which he had lived for most of his life. He firmly believed that he could be successful there. So, when he realized that I wasn't willing to leave, he stopped seeing me. We went our separate ways.

Eventually, though, he sent for me. He told me, "I would really love for you to be my wife. And I have decided to settle in Nigeria."

I accepted and was very happy. Before I left him that day, I prayed with my fiancé by my side: God, You are the Rock of Ages. Be the rock of our union in Jesus' name.

◆

One Sunday afternoon Paul said that he needed to talk to me, that he had something to tell me. I quickly answered, "You are reading my mind. I have something I want to tell you also." We agreed to meet on a chosen date and time.

At the meeting Paul talked first. He told me he had a daughter who was around three years old the last time he had seen her.

"What?!"

I was dumfounded, scared, sad, angry, speechless, and confused. When I was finally able to open my mouth, I said, "So, you are married?"

"I was never married."

"Then how could you have a daughter without marriage?"

Paul then told me he had made a mistake in life long before he accepted Christ. He said that mistake had cost him everything he had and ever worked for up to that point. It was not until he later came to Latter Rain Ministries and heard Pastor Bakare preaching on forgiveness that he got born again. At the end of the sermon Pastor had given an altar call for everybody that had been angry with one or two people. He asked everyone to come forward and forgive that other person no matter how terrible or painful it might seem to be so that God could start a new life in you. That day Paul walked to the altar, and Pastor prayed for him. God gave him a new heart to start all over again.

Paul went on to tell me that he had no clue where his daughter lived. All he knew was that her mother was married and had other children. Then, he said, "Now tell me what you wanted to tell me."

"I wanted to tell you that I have never known any man. I have been prayerfully waiting for marriage with the right man, one who had found favor with God, one who would be a crown to me. He has kept me this long, and I am a special daughter of whom God is very proud and jealous."

I was so confused. What was Paul expecting me to say to him about his daughter? Why had he waited to tell me until after I accepted his marriage proposal? I needed a word from God.

So, I set my concern before the Lord. I cried out to him, saying "I don't know how to be a stepmother. I have never seen how one acts. I don't know what to do..." And my conversation with my heavenly Father went on and on and on: "What if.....what if.....what if....what if..."

The Lord answered me: "You do not have to be a stepmom. All you have to do is accept her as your own daughter, take care and pray for her just like you would your own daughter." That was the Word of God to me. I decided to do exactly what God said do, and I was peaceful and happy again.

Paul and I then went to the marriage committee of Latter Rain Ministries, making our intentions known to the church.

◆

Latter Rain Ministries believes in marriage and the importance of starting out strong. That being the case, there is a marriage committee that approves/disapproves couples who are asking to be married within the church. All couples must attend multiple weeks of teaching lectures on marriage. In addition, there is prayer and counseling. If throughout the process nothing negative is found, then the committee approves the wedding and schedules a final interview to be held with Latter Rain's serving overseer, Pastor Tunde Bakare.

Well, the day came that we both had to be interviewed by Pastor Bakare. I was very nervous and shy as I sat with Paul in the pastor's office, facing him across the table. It did not matter that he had given us both a warm and gentle welcome.

The interview started with a simple prayer and then the questions started. The interview became so intense. Pastor was beginning to show some concern about me especially. That is when he decided to talk to each of us separately. Paul was asked to wait in the reception area. I was to be first.

My one-on-interview went something like this.

Pastor: Has Paul told you about his former relationship and his daughter?

Clara: Yes, Sir.

Pastor: And why have you decided to marry him?

Clara: Not for money. I can take care of myself. I have a job.

Pastor: I am not asking you about money. I want to know the real reason why you want to marry Paul.

Clara: I really love him. (crying)

Pastor: Well, said.

Then, he told me, and I quote, "Se omo pe Igbale ti afina Iyale wa ni orule fun Iyawo," which means "Do you realize that the same reason the first relationship was not successful is still alive, waiting for the new relationship?"

Clara: I have been concerned. I prayed about it and God promised that he would never leave me. He told me that he would always be there with me.

I could see that Pastor was still not convinced. I could see that he was worried about me. He then excused me and asked Paul to come inside.

Pastor's interview with Paul was longer than mine. The entire time I sat there wondering what was going on in the office. I hoped everything was fine. But all I could think of was what would happen if Pastor did not agree to our marrying.

When the door finally opened, there were no smiles. I was afraid what Pastor was going to say.

Pastor then told both of us to stay in the waiting room. He said that he needed to pray alone. So, we waited.

Paul asked what my interview session was like. I shared what had been said, and then he told me about his. Pastor had wanted to be sure he was serious about me, being very protective of his spiritual daughters.

We then became very quiet as we anxiously waited Pastor's verdict. Finally, his door opened. He invited us in and began to pray for us. He spoke blessings over us and decreed success in our union. After finishing, he told us that he had a sense that there would be a lot of difficulty in our way but that God had shown him that we would be successful, that we would overcome. Pastor then gave us his approval of our marriage but then went on to tell Paul over and over again to take care of his daughter.

After our interview with Pastor Bakare a date was set for the registry wedding, then the inter-tribal wedding, and finally the church wedding. I had waited so long and was so blessed. I knew God had answered my cry. The Lord had both prospered me on my job as well personally.

I finally had received the desire of my heart: a godly man who had obtained favor from the Lord. And although I had prayed and planned for that day, I could never have imagined the process I would have to go through to get there. But it was worth the wait because Paul was truly God's reward to me!

Chapter Nine

A Change of Plans

Marriage with God's man for me was wonderful just as I thought it would be. Actually, it was more, especially when God blessed us with a son just eleven months and six days after our wedding. How far I had come! My days were filled with the joy of both marriage and motherhood.

Then, my husband convinced me that he should travel to the United States. Our son was only seven months old at the time. What was to only have been a few months turned into a year. I missed my husband, do I decided to visit him in America.

Deciding to visit the United States and getting a visa are two very different things. However, God once again moved on my behalf. He provided a visa interview for me through somebody who knew somebody. And I was approved to travel. I was so excited.

◆

My visa included a transit stop a stop in Germany, so I decided to leave the airport and go into the city. I had some friends there that I wanted to visit. While out, I lost my passport or it was stolen from me. (That is something you never want to have happen!)

Eventually, I ended up in the Germany embassy. I, of course, had to call Paul in America. While we discussed my situation, he decided that I should file for a German visa. However, a few months turned into two years. My son and I never went home. We made our home in Germany while I completed the process for green card entry into the United States for both of us.

I had to laugh to myself when I realized all the plans I had made back in Nigeria. Could I be the same person who had actually told my husband that I would not marry him unless he promised to stay in Nigeria. How my plans had changed!

◆

My husband did not come to live with us in Germany but was able to visit a couple of times. I missed him so very much but knew that eventually we would be together. And even though I was without him, I reminded myself that God had promised to never leave me. I was safe in my heavenly Father's care.

However, I will be honest and say that my time in Germany was not easy. While there, I saw much that caused me to fear for my own marriage as well as question our decision to leave Nigeria. I saw wives cheating on their husbands who were either in Nigeria or other parts of the world. I also saw how men left everything they had in Nigeria to go abroad only to find out that the grass was not actually greener on the other side. Many of them regretted their actions. Some even became addicted to drugs and alcohol; a few of them ended up in jail; others even lost their lives in pursuit of their dreams.

Many of these sad stories had their root in falsehood, misconception, and sin. People would leave Nigeria, travel abroad, and come back home with cars and plenty of money. That, in and of itself, was not a problem. It was that others who saw them return did not know how these individuals had made their money did not matter — their wealth and the power and position that accompanied it was what drove them to also go abroad. They had not sought counsel; they had not sought God's will concerning their dream of leaving their nation for other countries. Instead, they had sold every-thing they had in pursuit of a dream, one that had no basis in reality. Once away, many realized too late that they had been better off at home. They had not understood that they had been living like kings and queens in their own country, a land filled with many natural resources (i.e., gold, oil, and an abundance of agriculture).

However, I knew that not everyone left Nigeria for the wrong reasons. I did see some who had taken the time to seek the Lord and prepare for what they would face when outside their own borders. They expressed a heartfelt calling to travel to other nations, and success was the result.

So, I had some decisions to make. I could either rely on myself or I could rely on the Lord. I could either give in to fear or stand in faith. I could either trust my husband to lead our family in the way we should go or try to make the deci-sions for myself. My plans had to be left in the dust; God's plans had to be allowed to grow and develop in me.

Proverbs 16:9
In his heart a man plans his course, but the LORD determines his steps.

Isaiah 55:8-9
"For my thoughts are not your thoughts, neither are your ways my ways," declares the Lord. "As

**the heavens are higher than the earth, so are my
ways higher than your ways and my thoughts than
your thoughts."**

After a very long wait I was going to join my husband, my
crown, in the States. However, my second child, a daughter,
had been born by the time all the necessary emigration
paperwork was processed. Therefore, the US government
approved a green card for both me and my son and issued an
American passport to my daughter.

Finally, the day came when the two children and I boarded
a plane. So much prayer, so many tears, so much frustration
to get to that point. We were emigrating to the United States
of America!

I thought once we arrived in America everything would
be okay. However, I still had some lessons to learn and some
adjustments to make. My loneliness threatened to steal my
joy and my dreams. I had been lonely in Nigeria when my
husband had left me with our newborn son, and I had been
even lonelier in Germany, where I had to learn the language
and a new culture. I had gone through so many trials and
much temptation in Europe those two years while waiting to
be cleared. But nothing had prepared me for the loneliness I
would experience upon my arrival in the US.

One day I began to think back to my marriage interview
with Pastor Bakare. I realized that I now better understood
why Pastor had been so worried about me and my future.
Sitting there, I said to myself, "I wish Pastor had told me that
I was going to be lonely in a strange country. Then, I would
have run away and never gotten married."

Little did I know that this new season of my life was another test, one which would prepare for my ultimate success. At that point I could not even begin to imagine anything but my loneliness; my dreams of wealth and success as a Nigerian businesswoman had become very dim.

The only thing that did keep me going was the knowledge that God was always faithful. He had promised that He would never leave or forsake me. Even though it did not feel like that was true, I knew it to be so. God had never let me down in the past, and I knew He would not do so now.

Deuteronomy 31:6
Be strong and courageous. Do not be afraid or terrified because of them, for the Lord your God goes with you; he will never leave you nor forsake you.

Joshua 1:5
No one will be able to stand up against you all the days of your life. As I was with Moses, so I will be with you; I will never leave you nor forsake you.

I came to America, full of the spirit of God and His Word. I had been equipped by my years at Latter Rain Ministries. I knew what it was to tap into the spirit realm through prayer, fasting, and the Word of God. My personal relationship with the Lord was a strong one, and I knew what it was to live in His presence.

However, living in America was somehow different. Everything I knew before about culture and business had to be adjusted. I was so very thankful for the training I had received when I worked at The Sheraton Towers, but I needed more. We needed more.

Just when I thought the loneliness would not end, just when I thought I would never get a breakthrough in this nation, the Lord met our need. He led us to a church whose mission it is to build lives with Kingdom purpose. They do this by stressing both spiritual and economic empowerment, believing that both are needed in order to transform our families, communities, and nations through Christ.

Apostle Jamie T. Pleasant PhD and his wife Pastor Kimberly Pleasant were those God had called for this purpose. God had given Apostle Pleasant the vision to establish a biblically based economic development initiative for the church. As a result, he had created programs in the church such as the Wealth Builders Investment Club (WBIC) that educates members how to invest in the stock market. He had also started the Institute of Entrepreneurship (IOE), where community members could earn a certificate in entrepreneurship after three months of comprehensive training on every aspect related to starting and owning a successful, competitive business. The church even offered SAT & PSAT prep courses for children between the ages of 13 -17 to fuel the potential success of all children.

My husband and I began to grow and develop in our new country. As we stayed under the teaching and encouragement of Pastor Pleasant, our faith grew and our dreams began to take shape. Seven years after finding our new church, the two of us were able to "retire" from corporate life in order to start our own business. In the process I found out that my dreams were coming to pass, just not in the way I had originally thought all those years before as a young woman in Nigeria. And I will have to say that God's plans for me and for Paul were far better than my own had been.

◆

92

One thing I have learned is this: God never stops amazing me. One day I was in my office when I received a phone call from my husband. He said, "Guess what? I am standing in front of Pastor Tunde Bakare." I could not believe my ears. I immediately jumped off my chair and started screaming and yelling. I had to stop and explain to my client what a miracle God had just done.

Once my husband and I had left Nigeria, we had lost touch with Pastor Bakare. All of our efforts to contact him had been fruitless. Thank God he had taught us to have a personal relationship with God and to pray our own way into the Holy of Holies, taking our petitions straight to the Lord instead of relying on him to do so. By doing that we had been able to survive all of our tests and trials but had sorely missed Pastor Bakare and his weekly spiritual influence in our lives.

What a joy it was to reconnect with our pastor and father in the Lord as well as Mrs. B and the family. As we began to share all that had happened in our lives, we found out that God had called Pastor Bakare to all nations to develop and restore churches to the biblical pattern. Our reunion was a sweet one, bringing so much revelation to our lives.

However, we were sincerely blessed that we were also able to reconnect with many pastors and friends we had known in Nigeria but had since moved abroad as well. Pastors Bank and Sharon Akinmola of World Outreach for all Nations were just the first of our many renewed relationships. (When we visit the church in Atlanta, we feel right at home.) We also were able to renew our acquaintance with Dr. James Iruofagar and his wife Pastor Faith Iruofagar of Glory Christian Center, who had emigrated from Lagos, Nigeria, to the United States as missionaries. (Their church is another home away from home for us.)

Our relationship with Dr. Bakare here in the States has also brought about our introduction to many new friends and ministries. We have met Dr. Jonathan David and his wife Helen of the Full Gospel Centre in Muar Johor, Malaysia. What a blessing their ministry has been to our lives! Also, it was a great honor when we were introduced to Dr. Delron Shirley and his wife Peggy of Teach All Nations ministry.

With the encouragement from men and women of God like those I have mentioned (and many that I have not) I continue to grow and develop through life's challenges. My plans have become more and more aligned with God's plans in the process. That is not to say that I have had to forego my dreams. No! I have just had to expand them and allow God to orchestrate their coming to pass instead of my trying to make them happen.

My life does look different — in fact, very different — than I pictured it all those many years ago as a girl and then as a young woman in Nigeria. But it is a good difference! I have truly learned that the Lord has my best interest at heart.

Ephesians 3:20-21
Now to him who us able to [carry out his purpose and] do immeasurably more [superabundantly, far and above] than all we [dare] ask or imagine [infinitely beyond our highest prayers, desires, thoughts, hopes, or dreams], according to his power that is at work within us, to him be glory... (NIV with extra material from AMP)

◆

Finally, another aspect of my life that is beyond what I could have ever asked, imagined, or thought is that of my involvement in athletics. When I was younger, running, playing, or being part of a sports team was never an option. There was always work to be done and no time for extra curricular activities. The same was true when I started my career.

Therefore, my physical endurance training began when I reached the United States. I would walking and or run slowly on my own especially when my heart was heavily burdened. I also would take long walks just to fellowship with (and complain to) God. Being outside, alone, I would cry out to Him, telling Him how I had no help and about how lonely and tired I was. It was in those times that I found that God would always refresh and comfort me so that by the time I reached home I would be energized—always filled to overflowing with new found strength, joy, wisdom about my situation, and new ideas.

My walks for comfort turned into real athletic training at some point along the way. I am not sure when. But the most interesting part is that my training led to the strengthening of my faith and endurance in the Spirit.

I think it first began with my watching the Peachtree Road Race. Each year my desire to be a part of such an event strengthened my desire to get serious about my pastime. I found myself praying that I would someday be running in it.

Then, I was introduced to the Atlanta track club. I became more serious as I began to diligently train. This eventually led to my running in my 1st Peachtree Road Race in 2003, and I have been running it ever since. Now I run in several races each year, including various 10k and half marathon events as well as Atlanta's full marathon (26.2 miles), beginning with NIKI's Atlanta Women's 5k in March.

God had taught me great lessons (both natural and spiritual) over my many years of running. However, he has specifically spoken to me about The Race that all Christians are running. In this life we run to receive a crown in heaven, to be welcomed home, not with the congratulation of friends, family, or fellow participants but with a "Welcome home, faithful servant in the Kingdom of God." Just as I look for the finish line of each and every road race, so I look for the finishing line of my life's race where I expect to receive a medal from my King.

Problems, pain, worry, and anxiety can all cause a believer to fall by the road side and not finish the race of life well. This year I learned that the struggles and trials I experience along my way are preparation for the next level of spiritual growth and attainment. If all of those trials are not properly fought and won through the grace of God, my finishing well is put in jeopardy.

In closing, the quality of your training—especially for a full marathon race—is the key factor in your overall success. You can not wait until the day of the race to start; you must have been planning, preparing, and training all along the way. If not, you are going to be sidelined and unable to finish the race. As a believer, I must keep that principle uppermost in my mind. I must continue to feed on the Word daily; I must keep my prayer life a healthy and vibrant one; I must make sure I place the Lord and my relationship with him as the first priority in my life.

If I am to "finish my course with joy" as the Apostle Paul has declared then I must stay conditioned and ready. I can not afford to take a break or be sidetracked by life's problems. And neither can you!

So, I challenge you to learn the same life lessons that I have:

God loves you with an everlasting love,
God will protect and keep you,
God will make all things work together for your benefit,
God is the one who justifies and defends you,
God will give you your heart's desires,
God will never leave you; He will never forsake you,

God has a plan for your life—better than anything you yourself could think up, and Diligence, hard work, and training are absolute necessities for a successful finish.

If you do, I promise that you will never be the same. And there will be nothing that will stop you from crossing the finish line of your life in victory!

Chapter Ten

No Progress without Process

My early days in the United States of America, as I said earlier, were very lonely although I was very busy. I eventually faced the highest degree of trials, tribulations, and temptations that I had ever come up against. Even my faith, my love for Lord, and the standard of my relationship with God were tested.

Today, looking back on the process through which God had taken me, I cannot but agreed with Dr. Tunde Bakare when he repeatedly says "No Progress without Process". For, the more I look back and study the step by step process that God had taken me through in order to be where I am today my mouth hangs wide open in awe of God. To see how He has put the pieces of the puzzle together causes me to stop where I am, throw up my hands and worship Him. And I am sure that as you have read the story of my life you too have been able to see how God has progressively taken me from one place to another, from one level to another.

As a little girl, I became aware of God and His infinite mercy. I prayed and prayed, asking Him to change my circumstances. I wanted so much more than I had—education, wealth, fame, a better life for me and my children. However, as I grew in the Lord, I began to realize that I wanted all of those things but I wanted something else more—to be in line with His will. I desired that His Name alone might be glorified, in my life...and in my death.

What I did not understand was that when we pray to God for a reason or a purpose we do not have the slightest idea how God is going to get us there or what the process will be in order for us to reach our goals while giving all the glory to God. Some of us want a change in our situation, and we want it now. We pay little attention to the process, even sometimes trying to thwart the process in order to get where we are going, faster.

However, when life goals are met prematurely or through means other than what God approves, men (and women) often become arrogant. We sometimes forget that God is the One who made us, keeps us, blesses us, and places us where He wills. Even when one of life's storms comes our way, we forget to turn to God and instead search for answers in everything but God—drugs, alcohol, sex, psychics, or human counselors.

Instead, we must become like King Solomon. The man who is said to be the wisest of all time found that everything is meaningless without God. (See Ecclesiastes.) Would we be quick to understand and live by that truth!

◆

Even I can now appreciate aspects of my life when I see it through the lens of process. For example, my having to take care of my uncle, his home, and his children while going to school...helped to prepare me to be a successful wife and mother while remaining a businesswoman. For that preparation—for that process—I am thankful.

Early on in my life it became my normal lifestyle to wake up early in the morning, dress myself and two kids, clean up the house, and make breakfast for the family all before I walked out the door to "start" my day. Leaving after a full day of work to pick up the children from school, oversee homework, cook dinner, read bedtime stories, and work on school projects all before doing my own work...normal. Seeing to everyone else's needs before my own...normal. Fitting in laundry and housework around family times...normal.

Now, I rejoice and praise God because I serve my family out of love, not compulsion. I do laundry in the privacy of my own home instead of going to the river and back. I cook meals in a kitchen over which I am in charge. I clean because I want to make our house a home not because I will be beaten if everything does not pass inspection.

It is highly rewarding to see my husband and children excel. I see my husband taking his place as a respected, prosperous businessman. I see my children's names on the straight "A" honor rolls and am so very proud of them and their achievements. I can see my true spirit in them as they mature and take my dreams to the next level. Their success has become a reward to me.

Today, I am no longer the young girl who feels trapped. Rather I am a woman of God with a husband of worth and children of distinction who is able to give God the glory in and through all things because I have seen where His process takes me. I have found Him to be faithful. I have experienced the joy of allowing Him to lead and guide me even in the midst of horrible circumstances. He always knows the best path to take me where I am going, and He always makes a way for me even when there seems to be no way in the natural. And He will do the same for you!

I strive to become that virtuous woman of which King Lemuel writes in Proverbs. I desire to be someone whose character is her calling card, a wife who supports her husband in all he does, a homemaker who is diligent, a businesswoman who prospers, a believer who cares for those who are less fortunate, a lady of strength and dignity, and a mother whose children rise up and call her blessed. This is what brings me pure joy, true contentment, and a sense of accomplishment. However, I will only become that woman as I submit to God's process. For, remember there is no progress without process. I have learned this to be true, and I know you will as well.

Clara, mother & brothers

Proverb 31:10-31 (NIV)

A wife of noble character who can find? She is worth far more than rubies.

Her husband has full confidence in her and lacks nothing of value.

She brings him good, not harm, all the days of her life.

She selects wool and flax and works with eager hands.

She is like the merchant ships, bringing her food from afar.

She gets up while it is still dark; she provides food for her family and portions for her servant girls.

She considers a field and buys it; out of her earnings she plants a vineyard.

She sets about her work vigorously; her arms are strong for her tasks.

She sees that her trading is profitable, and her lamp does not go out at night.

In her hand she holds the distaff and grasps the spindle with her fingers.

She opens her arms to the poor and extends her hands to the needy.

When it snows, she has no fear for her household; for all of them are clothed in scarlet.

She makes coverings for her bed; she is clothed in fine linen and purple.

Her husband is respected at the city gate, where he takes his seat among the elders of the land.

She makes linen garments and sells them, and supplies the merchants with sashes.

She is clothed with strength and dignity; she can laugh at the days to come.

She speaks with wisdom, and faithful instruction is on her tongue.

She watches over the affairs of her household and does not eat the bread of idleness.

Her children arise and call her blessed; her husband also, and he praises her:

"Many women do noble things, but you surpass them all."

Charm is deceptive, and beauty is fleeting; but a woman who fears the LORD is to be praised.

Give her the reward she has earned, and let her works bring her praise at the city gate.

Proverb 31:10-31 (MSG)

A good woman is hard to find, and worth far more than diamonds.

Her husband trusts her without reserve, and never has reason to regret it.

Never spiteful, she treats him generously all her life long.

She shops around for the best yarns and cottons, and enjoys knitting and sewing.

She's like a trading ship that sails to faraway places and brings back exotic surprises.

She's up before dawn, preparing breakfast for her family and organizing her day.

She looks over a field and buys it, then, with money she's put aside, plants a garden.

First thing in the morning, she dresses for work, rolls up her sleeves, eager to get started.

She senses the worth of her work, is in no hurry to call it quits for the day.

She's skilled in the crafts of home and hearth, diligent in homemaking.

She's quick to assist anyone in need, reaches out to help the poor.

She doesn't worry about her family when it snows; their winter clothes are all mended and ready to wear.

She makes her own clothing, and dresses in colorful linens and silks.

Her husband is greatly respected when he deliberates with the city fathers.

She designs gowns and sells them, brings the sweaters she knits to the dress shops.

Her clothes are well-made and elegant, and she always faces tomorrow with a smile.

When she speaks she has something worthwhile to say, and she always says it kindly.

She keeps an eye on everyone in her household, and keeps them all busy and productive.

Her children respect and bless her; her husband joins in with words of praise:

"Many women have done wonderful things, but you've outclassed them all!"

Charm can mislead and beauty soon fades. The woman to be admired and praised is the woman who lives in the Fear-of-God.

Give her everything she deserves! Festoon her life with praises!

Chapter Eleven

Jobs Are Not Scarce; Faithful Men Are

D r. Tunde Bakare of Latter Rain Ministries, Lagos, Nigeria, and Church Development Group, USA, has been known to say, "Jobs are not scarce; faithful men are." The reality of that statement became very real to me when I began my search for my 1st managerial job in America. If I had not been faithful, I would not have been hired or kept on as an employee.

A management position was open. I thought I was the best qualified, most experienced, and most suitable for the job. In addition, I knew it would be good for my family schedule. But I was wrong! At the final interview I was told that I was not the fastest in moving from point A to B, so I was disqualified. That was strange to me. I did not understand, and I definitely did not agree.

I went home to my husband and began telling him that the people were very mean and wicked. Expecting Paul to be on my side, I was surprised when he disagreed with me. He then explained that a manager in America must not only be able to think fast but must also be able to multitask — doing two, three, or even four things at one time.

Paul demonstrated this to me by putting it in a context I would understand: my home. He likened it to my cooking, cleaning, taking phone calls, welcoming guests, smiling at all times, and much more for a minimum of eight hours a day without slowing. I had to admit that I did not think I could do that without fainting; I knew I did not have that kind of physical stamina. He said, "Then you're not ready to be a manager."

I had studied management. I was a natural born leader. I knew I would do a good job if given the chance. However, I suddenly realized that I was lacking the speed and physical stamina necessary to make it as a manager in the United States.

The answer: I went back to my husband and asked for his help. I wanted to know what I could do to become better. What's more, I never questioned him and his methods. I knew it was time for a change although it was not easy or comfortable in the beginning.

As my trainer, Paul started with my running on the spot with five pound weights tied to each foot. Then, I graduated to running up and down our street. After some time my husband had me wear weights in my shoes to work each day. The result: any time I took the weights off my feet, I became very light and began to work faster.

In Nigeria I had walked at a steady pace, never in a hurry for anything. I qualified as one who was described as "Arin gbere bi eni egbendun, Egbe odun wa ola Oluwa lombe lara wa" by close friends. This means that although you walk, you do so like you have a pain in your side although you do not have pain.

I loved it when I started getting results; I began working faster and smarter. However, the most important result was that I was hired for a management position with another company, where I was told that I was the most qualified candidate in all aspects of the job. My faithfulness to train and prepare had made the difference (with the help of my husband who believed in me).

As you have probably guessed from reading my story, I have never been one to sit back and rest on my achievements. I am always striving for more, for better. So, it will be no surprise to you that after two years at my first management position and upon hearing of another company where women were rarely hired as managers because of the work load, I decided I needed a new challenge. I asked about the salary possibilities and when I was told that it was almost double what I was being paid, I went and applied. My goal was to change the odds, to prove that a woman could not only be hired but could make it to the coveted management level.

I was hired as a manager in training as that particular company does not hire managers from outside the company. Every person who desires a management position must train, pass a written test, and then successfully complete a series of interviews prior to becoming a manager. I made my goal – I made it to management! Once again, my hard work and faithfulness had paid off.

I worked the opening shift for two years. That meant my getting up at 3 a.m. and then leaving home around 3:30 in order to open the store at 4. I was never late, not once.

Eventually, I was trusted with my own store key. The day it was presented to me, I received a beautiful floral arrangement and card signed by all of the employees. I had never felt so valued and trusted.

In the end I had to quit because my children were suffering. Also, my husband was already in top management at his company and was extremely busy. So, I made the decision to step down in order to better support my family. However, my stepping down did not mean that I was planning to not work altogether. I just needed a position that would be more flexible, allowing me to properly care for my family. *And guess what?* The Lord led me to the right management job, one that fit my needs but provided me with the challenges I needed to continue to grow and develop.

Then, six years later and with a tremendous amount of added experience, I finally registered my own business. My dream came true—even though property management is far different than my original café and catering idea that I had so many years ago in Nigeria. What's more, it is far better than I ever imagined! God has so faithfully led me down His path in order for me to reach my heart's desire. So, in closing, if you trust the Lord, if you walk in obedience to His commands and if you prove yourself faithful, you too will achieve your dream.

Appendix A

Work for the Lord

1 Colossians 3:23-24
Whatever you do, work at it with all your heart, as working for the Lord, not for men, since you know that you will receive an inheritance from the Lord as a reward. It is the Lord Christ you are serving.

What a scripture to live! Although not easy, it is something I am very conscious of each time I am given an opportunity to do anything. *Yes, I mean what I said.* Anything at all! I always work and aim at excellence in all that I do, knowing full well that God Himself is my rewarder.

There is no room in my life for me to be either idle or spend more hours than necessary on an assignment. As a result, excellence is always my goal, not to get ahead at all costs or receive a favorable review from a superior. *Why?* I trust that God Himself will give me my evaluation and care for me better than any boss. Therefore, if I am unable to convince the Lord of my faithfulness or diligence at work, I might as well forget going for a promotion or raise.

However, as hardworking and excellence oriented as I am, I have found that there is still more. As a Christian I have been called to walk a higher path, one that is narrow. How I behave on the job (whether I am working for myself or someone else) is of the utmost importance. Not only will it determine how well I do but it will also determine the kind of witness I am for the God I serve.

Appendix B

A Christian Employee's Motto

Always go to God for the grace and ability to discern and solve problems. Revelation of the secret and hidden things is a gift of God. (Matt. 13:14-15; Eph. 1)

Be a team player. I learned this by studying Jesus' instructions to His disciples: "the leader among you shall be the least". Doing this will help you relate better with your associates on all levels. (Lk. 22:26)

Demonstrate skills, accuracy, and speed. Make the highest quality product possible. You can not be lazy and expect your employees to be hard working: *whatever you sow, you shall reap.*

Encourage those around you on a regular basis.

During interview and selection you have to be able to clearly communicate your expectations. Make sure prospective employees understand their responsibilities.

Always maintain a high level of customer service.

Do whatever it takes to get along with everyone, no matter their background. Never discriminate!

Appendix C

A Few Questions to Ponder

*C*an *you be trusted at your work?* If not, I have a few suggestions for you to consider:

Get to work at least 10 minutes earlier than scheduled.

Answer a call for help on your day off.

Use the time and hour allocated to you efficiently.

Work for a minimum of four weeks straight without calling in sick.

Tell the truth. Don't call your boss and say you or your child is sick if that is not the case.

Are you at the top of the "keep at all costs" list at work? Or will you be one of the first to go when your company experiences a difficult time? Your work ethic will be the primary determining factor when someone is deciding which list you are on. When times get tough, your faithfulness and reliability will be remembered and factored into decisions.

Would those who surround you on a daily basis (i.e., your coworkers, your boss, your neighbor, your child's teacher, the lady in the grocery store, etc.) be able to tell that you are a Christian? Or would they be surprised to find out that you call yourself a Christian? We are called to be salt and light in this world. People are watching! So, make them thirsty for Jesus. Shine so brightly that it will be obvious that you are a child of the King.

Notes

Chapter Seven

chairman of the wedding – in the Nigerian culture this person is someone who is greatly respected. Being asked to be a chairman by the bride and groom is a great honor.

Postscript

Inow live in Atlanta, Georgia with my husband who is my crown and joy. We have three beautiful children who make every day an adventure.

I decided to write this book as a token of my gratitude to God. It is to Him alone that all the glory, honor, and praise is due. He has done great things in me and my life, and I shall be forever thankful.

Through my journey in life I have been able to meet with many great women who are called to faithfulness in serving God. God has given me many opportunities to be around them; they have ministered to me and have been a great inspiration in my life.

I have noticed that all successful women of God have certain things in common that are not common traits. We can all learn from them and their lives. That being the case, please look for my second book, which is entitled, *Woman You are Not Alone*. It celebrates womanhood and calls all women to victory.

Author Contact Information

Clara Stephens
Address~~~ P.O.Box 1278
Winder, Georgia 30680
Phone: (678) 231-4460
email: clarastephens08@aol.com

Printed in the United States
218523BV00002B/2/P

9 781607 917762